AROUND THE BRANCH LINES

No. 2
GREAT WESTERN

Plate 1:   The last days at Kington; a scene of dereliction on 9th August 1962, as the weeds start to take over the platforms. Passenger services ceased to operate on 8th February 1955 and the line closed completely on 28th September 1964.

AROUND THE BRANCH LINES

No. 2
GREAT WESTERN

Chris Gammell

Oxford Publishing Company

Typesetting by:
Aquarius Typesetting Services, New Milton, Hants.

Printed in Great Britain by:
Biddles Ltd., Guildford, Surrey.

From Aberystwyth, British Railways' only narrow-gauge
passenger trains climb through twelve miles of magnificent
Rheidol Valley scenery to Devil's Bridge and its famous
Falls - a ride to be enjoyed and remembered.

FURTHER READING
Great Western Branch Line Books by Oxford Publishing Co.

The Yeulmpton Branch	A. R. Kingdom
The Watlington Branch	J. Holden
The Princetown Branch	A. R. Kingdom
Lines to Avonmouth	M. Vincent
The Kingsbridge Branch	K. Williams & D. Reynolds
The Faringdon Branch	A. Vaughan
Calne Branch	G. Tanner
The Bridport Branch	B. L. Jackson & M. J. Tattershall
Cleobury Mortimer &	W. Smith & K. Beddoes
Ditton Priors Light Railway	
The Turnchapel Branch	A. R. Kingdom
The Woodstock Branch	R. Lingard
The Ashburton Branch	A. R. Kingdom

ACKNOWLEDGEMENTS
The author and publisher wish to acknowledge the assistance
rendered by K. Bill and David Soggee in checking the manu-
script, Neville Dexter Ltd., for photographic services and
Deborah Dudley for secretarial work. The maps have been
drawn by Edwin Wilmshurst.

Published by:
Oxford Publishing Co.
Link House,
West Street,
POOLE, Dorset

BIBLIOGRAPHY

Title	Author(s)	Publisher	Date
Cambrian Railways	R. W. Kidner	Oakwood Press	1954
Brecon & Merthyr Railway	D. S. Barrie	Oakwood Press	1957
Midland & South Western Junction Railway	T. B. Sands	Oakwood Press	1959
History of the Great Western Railway	C. R. Clinker/ MacDermot	Ian Allan	1964
British Branch Lines	H. A. Vallance	Batsford	1965
North Pembroke & Fishguard Railway	J. P. Morris	Oakwood Press	1969
Taff Vale Railway	D. S. Barrie	Oakwood Press	1969
Cambrian Railways	R. Christiansen & R. W. Miller	David & Charles	1971
Mawddy, Van and Kerry Railways	L. Cozens	Oakwood Press	1972
Rhymney Railway	D. S. Barrie	Oakwood Press	1973
Whitland & Cardigan Railway	M. R. C. Price	Oakwood Press	1976
Oxford, Worcester & Wolverhampton Railway	Jenkins & Quale	Oakwood Press	1977
Banbury & Cheltenham Railway	J. H. Russell	OPC	1977
Guide to Closed Railways in Britain 1948–75		BLS	1977
Manchester & Milford Railway	J. S. Holden	Oakwood Press	1979
Guide to Steam Railways, Great Britain	Awdrey/Cooke	Pelham	1979
Regional History Railways Great Britain Vol. II	P. Baughan	David & Charles	1980
Rail Atlas of Great Britain	S. K. Baker	OPC	1980
Preserved Locomotives	H. C. Casserley	Ian Allan	1980
Passengers No More	G. Daniels & L. Dench	Ian Allan	1980
Railway Magazine, Railway World, and Branch Line News			Various issues

Plate 2:   The Great Western restored. Ex-GWR pannier tank, No. 6412 sizzles outside the commodious goods shed on the revitalized West Somerset Railway at Minehead on 15th April 1976. The former Minehead branch closed to passengers on 4th January 1971. On 28th March 1976 the West Somerset Railway was formally opened from Minehead to Blue Anchor: a Great Western branch line saved.

INTRODUCTION

In the 1950s a passenger waiting for a train could stand on the platform at Paddington and watch the 'all steam' comings and goings of the Western Region, and would be safe in the knowledge that, but for a few experimental locomotives, shunters and railcars, this steam empire stretched all the way down the line to Penzance. Every station echoed to the snorts and clanks and distinctive crowing whistles of Great Western engines. In 1955, British Railways announced the modernization plan. This started to take effect in the early 1960s and by 1965, all steam power was abolished on the Western Region. During the last ten years of steam on the region I travelled about the system photographing the everyday scene as well as the more sobering last days on doomed branch lines.

In this volume I have included pictures of last days on branch lines as well as pictures of closure notices, tickets, labels and other relics, to create the atmosphere of the British branch line in its final days. I have included, pictorially, most lines, but not all, but every line on the former GWR system is accounted for in the appropriate introduction to the relevant county. This book includes new photographs of GWR branch lines and contains more information than the previous book, written by me; *Great Western Branch Lines 1955–1965*, now out of print. I have also included some transition pictures or 'before and after' views of the West Somerset branch as not all Great Western branch lines are dead and buried, some having been restored, now operating as preserved light railways open to the public during the summer months.

There is no doubt that the Great Western went in for branch lines in a big way, even more so than the others of the 'Big Four'. The Great Western Railway did its utmost to combat bus and motor car competition. In the 1920s and 1930s, many halts were opened, stations were unstaffed and tickets were issued on the train by the guard. The guard issued bell punch tickets just like a bus conductor. Specialized locomotives and rolling stock were also constructed for branch line use and the new halts were at rail level. This meant that the passengers had to alight from special fold-down steps operated by the guard, a copy of American practice. The rolling stock was built for push-pull working and some auto trailers were actually built in 1954: the last non-standard vehicles built on British Railways.

The halts were built out of old sleepers or carried the ubiquitous GWR corrugated iron 'pagoda', usually lit by a flickering oil lamp at night, a job that had to be done by the guard. The guard from the last train of the day would have to extinguish the lamps at night. I found the most amazing relics on Great Western branch lines, such as passengers' luggage labels, which were kept in racks in the parcels offices of small stations, which had been untouched since the lines were built and were, quite literally, hundreds of years old! The more that one looked at the branch lines of the Great Western Railway, the more one discovered!

C. J. Gammell
London
1983

Plate 3: The somewhat lengthy platform at Staines West engulfs the tiny two car diesel multiple unit on 11th October 1958. The Staines branch passenger service ceased on 29th March 1965 and was, until recently, intact, but since January 1981, the section from Colnbrook to Staines has been closed as a new spur has now been put in from the former Staines Southern Railway line to serve the goods terminal.

NORTH & CENTRAL WALES

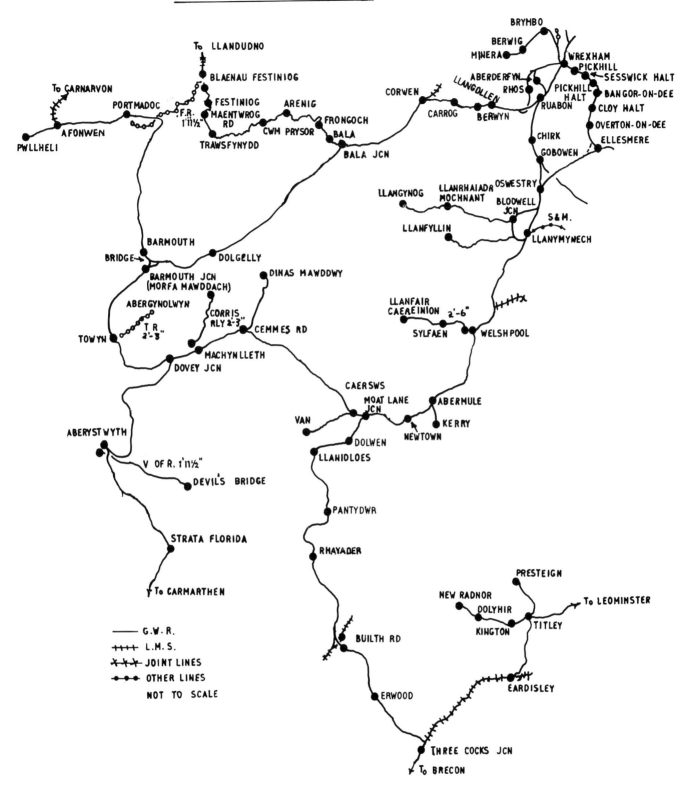

To LLANDUDNO

To CARNARVON

BLAENAU FESTINIOG

PORTMADOC
F.R. 1'11½"
FESTINIOG
MAENTWROG RD
ARENIG
FRONGOCH
CWM PRYSOR
BALA
TRAWSFYNYDD
BALA JCN

AFONWEN

PWLLHELI

BRYHBO
BERWIG
MINERA
WREXHAM
PICKHILL
SESSWICK HALT
ABERDERFYN
BANGOR-ON-DEE
RHOS
PICKHILL HALT
CLOY HALT
RUABON
OVERTON-ON-DEE
CHIRK
ELLESMERE
GOBOWEN

CORWEN
LLANGOLLEN
CARROG
BERWYN

OSWESTRY
LLANGYNOG
LLANRHAIADR MOCHNANT
BLOOWELL JCN
S & M.
LLANFYLLIN
LLANYMYNECH

BARMOUTH
BRIDGE
DOLGELLY
BARMOUTH JCN
(MORFA MAWDDACH)
DINAS MAWDDWY

LLANFAIR CAEREINION
2'-6"
ABERGYNOLWYN
CORRIS RLY 2'-3"
SYLFAEN
WELSHPOOL
T R. 2'-3"
CEMMES RD
TOWYN
MACHYNLLETH
DOVEY JCN

CAERSWS
ABERMULE
MOAT LANE JCN
VAN
KERRY
NEWTOWN
ABERYSTWYTH
DOLWEN
LLANIDLOES
V OF R. 1'11½"
DEVIL'S BRIDGE

STRATA FLORIDA
PANTYDWR

To CARMARTHEN
RHAYADER

PRESTEIGN
NEW RADNOR
To LEOMINSTER
DOLYHIR
KINGTON
TITLEY

BUILTH RD

ERWOOD
EARDISLEY

THREE COCKS JCN
To BRECON

———— G.W.R.
+++++ L.M.S.
×××× JOINT LINES
•—•—• OTHER LINES

NOT TO SCALE

The railways in Central Wales ran through fine scenery but through sparsely-populated countryside. The Cambrian Railways was the principal company operating in Central Wales and operated standard as well as narrow gauge lines. The Great Western absorbed the Cambrian Railway at the railway Grouping which was effective from 1923. This amalgamation of the Cambrian and Great Western railways added considerably to the GWR's mileage in Wales. Some minor railways escaped the Grouping of 1923 so the area was still potted with minor narrow gauge and light railways after 1923, and even after the 1948 nationalization. Thus the area has always been a fascinating part of Britain to visit and even today, new narrow gauge railways are being constructed.

The most spectacular of the Great Western branch lines to be seen in North Wales was the lengthy line from Bala Junction, on the Ruabon to Barmouth line, to Blaenau Festiniog; a distance of 25 miles. The line passed through some grand scenery and one could photograph trains running along the mountainside with Snowdon, the highest mountain in Wales, in the background. The branch opened from Bala Junction to Bala on 1st April 1868 and the section on to Festiniog on 10th September 1883. The final part of the line from Festiniog to Blaenau ran over the trackbed of a narrow gauge line formerly 1 ft. 11½ in. gauge, a rare instance in Britain of narrow gauge being converted to standard. Connection at Blaenau Festiniog was made with the former London & North Western Railway branch from Llandudno Junction. The views from the train might have been spectacular but passenger traffic was sparse, to say the least and the last passenger train ran on 22nd January 1961 in abysmal weather. The line was closed completely from 30th January 1961 and the lower part of the branch was flooded for a hydroelectric scheme. The top part of the line from Trawsfynydd to Blaenau Festiniog was reopened on 24th April 1964 to serve Tranwsfynydd Power-Station.

The Ruabon to Barmouth Junction line (Morfa Mawddach) closed to passenger traffic on 18th January 1965 and to all traffic from Bala Junction to Barmouth Junction. The Llangollen to Bala Junction line closed to all traffic on 14th December 1964 as a result of flooding, and the Llangollen to Ruabon line closed to all traffic on 1st April 1968.

The branch lines from Wrexham to Rhos and Wrexham to Berwig closed to passengers on 1st January 1931 and the Brymbo West to Minera line closed to all traffic on 1st January 1972. Aberderfyn Goods closed on 25th October 1954. The Great Western operated a cross-country branch line from Wrexham Central, connecting with the LNER to Ellesmere. This former Cambrian line, worked by auto trains and 14XX class tank engines, ran through parts of Flintshire and had some delightfully-named halts such as Sesswick, Pickhill and Cloy. The line was opened in 1895 as the Wrexham & Ellesmere Railway but was worked by the Cambrian Railway. The passenger service was withdrawn on 10th September 1962. A curious feature of the line was a through service from Manchester to Aberystwyth which was a Cambrian and Great Central venture. The trains ran by this route prior to the Grouping, an avoiding line being put in at Ellesmere for this purpose. The Wrexham & Ellesmere line also closed to passengers during World War II, from 10th June 1940 until 6th May 1946. The line closed to all traffic from Pickhill to Ellesmere on 10th September 1962.

The Cambrian Railway opened an 8¾ mile branch to Llanfyllin on 10th April 1863, this line lasting until 18th January 1965 when the Whitchurch to Welshpool passenger service ceased. The Llanfyllin branch closed to all traffic on this day. Nearby, north of Llanfyllin, was the Tanat Valley Light Railway also owned by the Cambrian Railway. The Tanat Valley Light Railway was opened on 5th January 1904 with four passenger trains per day between Oswestry and Llangynog. The Cambrian took over the Tanat Valley Light Railway in 1921 and passenger services ceased on 15th January 1951, freight traffic finishing between Llanrhaiadr and Llangynog on 1st July 1952. Freight traffic eventually ceased from Llanrhaiadr to Blodwell Junction on 6th January 1964.

A famous railway in the Shropshire/Welsh borders area was the narrow gauge Welshpool & Llanfair Railway, a Great Western narrow gauge railway which still operates today as a tourist line. The line was built to a 2 ft. 6 in. gauge and terminated outside Welshpool's Cambrian Station, the line opening on 9th March 1903. The line was worked by the Cambrian and used two attractive-looking 0-6-0 side tanks built by Beyer Peacock named *The Earl* and *The Countess*. This rural narrow gauge line, built for local traffic only, soon succumbed to rival bus competition, and passenger services were withdrawn on 9th February 1931. Strangely enough, freight traffic continued until 1956, the last train running on 3rd November. This was too much for many enthusiasts and a preservation movement was started with eventual success. On 6th April 1963 the Welshpool & Llanfair Railway re-opened over part of the line and, by 1972, it was operating a service from Llanfair to Sylfaen. Extension through to Welshpool was completed on 18th July 1981 with a brand new terminal at Raven Square, Welshpool. Over the years, new additions to the locomotive and rolling stock have been acquired including locomotives imported from overseas. The one time empty station yard at Llanfair Caereinion is now crammed full of 'goodies' for visiting tourists to view.

Another narrow gauge line in the area, which unfortunately failed to be preserved, was the 2 ft. 3 in. gauge Corris Railway. Opened on 4th July 1888, the line was used by the slate industry as was the nearby Talyllyn Railway. The Corris Railway was purchased by the GWR in 1930. The passenger services were withdrawn on 1st January 1931 but freight continued until 20th August 1948. The line was damaged by floods and dismantled by British Railways in 1950. The Corris Railway has a preservation society who are hoping to relay some of the track and start a passenger service once they have a Light Railway Order.

A standard gauge branch line ran from Dinas Mawddy to Cemmes Road, which was situated on the Cambrian main line. The branch was opened on 1st October 1867 and closed to all traffic on 8th April 1908. The line was re-opened on 31st July 1911 and worked by the Cambrian Railway, passenger services ceasing on 1st January 1931 and the last freight train running on 5th September 1950. The Cambrian had a short 3¾ mile branch from Abermule to Kerry which opened on 2nd March 1863 and which was closed to passengers on 9th February 1931 and to freight on 1st May 1956.

The Great Western acquired the Van Railway on 1st January 1923; a line that had been worked by the Cambrian and which had been opened originally in 1871 for trains to the lead mines of Van. The GWR closed the line on 4th November 1940 and removed the track in 1941.

The railway to Devil's Bridge is still in operation being British Rail's only all steam-worked line. Although only 1 ft. 11½ in. gauge and with three locomotives, passenger traffic is still increasing every year. The locomotives are painted BR rail green, GWR Brunswick green and the original 'Stroudley' yellow. British Rail have spent a certain amount of time and money on improving the terminal facilities. The Vale of Rheidol Railway was opened to Devil's Bridge in 1902, as an independent company; a distance of 11¾ miles. The Cambrian took over the Rheidol company in 1913 and it became part of the Great Western Railway at the Grouping. As a result, the Western Region of British Railways inherited this narrow gauge railway in 1948.

In the eastern part of Powys, on the Worcestershire and Herefordshire borders are the remains of the Presteign and New Radnor branches. The Presteign branch closed to passengers on 5th February 1951 and to freight on 28th September 1964. The New Radnor line to Kington closed to passengers on 5th February 1951, and the Dolyhir to New Radnor section closed on 31st December 1951 to freight.

The Mid Wales line from Moat Lane Junction to Three Cocks closed to passengers on 31st December 1962 and also on that date from Llanidloes to Three Cocks to all traffic. Moat Lane to Llanidloes closed to freight on 2nd October 1967. The one time Manchester & Milford Railway was built with the intention of meeting the Mid Wales Railway at Llanidloes but only got as far as Strata Florida where the proprietors decided to change direction and head for Aberystwyth. A line was constructed from Llanidloes to Llangurig but was never opened.

Plates 4 & 5: BR Standard Class 4MT 4-6-0s took over from ex-GWR engines during the last years of the Ruabon to Barmouth line. The class was built from 1951 to 1956 and several examples remain to be seen on the preserved railways of Britain. *(Above)* No. 75026 arrives at Berwyn, seen here demoted to 'halt' status, in November 1964, a few weeks before the closure of the 54½ mile long line. *(Below)* No. 75020, of the same class, eases into Carrog and picks up a few passengers for Barmouth on this once busy cross-country GWR route.

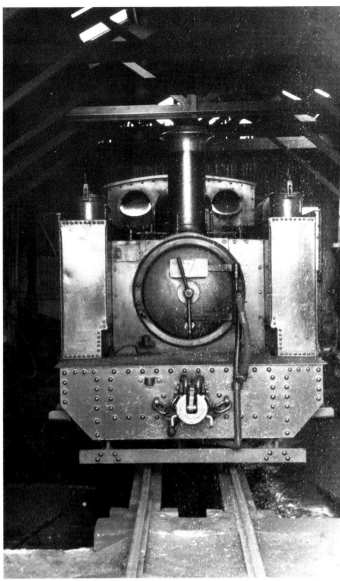

Plates 6 to 8: Scenes at Aberystwyth old shed with *(top left)* No. 9 *Prince of Wales*, the oldest locomotive on the line built for the opening of the line in 1902. *(Top right)* No. 7 *Owain Glyndwr* was built in 1923. Both locomotives were photographed on 23rd June 1956. *(Below)* A view taken down the valley, from near the summit showing how this 1 ft. 11½ in. gauge line winds its way up the mountainside. *(Photograph by Valentines). (Below left)* A Taff Vale label to Aberystwith shows the round about route a traveller would have to take from South Wales to get to Aberystwith (note the spelling!) for his annual holiday.

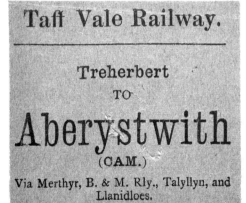

Taff Vale Railway.

Treherbert
TO
Aberystwith
(OAM.)

Via Merthyr, B. & M. Rly., Talyllyn, and Llanidloes.

RHEIDOL VALLEY, DEVIL'S BRIDGE.

29 JJ

Plate 9: A view from the small footbridge near the station at Devil's Bridge on 23rd June 1956, showing locomotive No. 8 *Llywelyn* taking water before pushing the stock back into the station.

Plate 10: Dolgelly, in Novem[...]
1964 with Class 2MT 2-6-0 [...]
46521 on a Barmouth local s[...]
about to depart tender fi[...]
Dolgelly used to be the bound[...]
station between the GWR [...]
the Cambrian Railway syst[...]
The line closed to all traffic [...]
18th January 1965. This lo[...]
motive can still be seen to[...]
running on the Severn Va[...]
Railway.

Plate 11: Rhayader, on the Mid Wales line in August 1962, with a grubby Class 2, 2-6-0 with equally dirty Hawksworth stock. A difficult subject to photograph as the train is coming out of the sun. Note the ornate water columns which are not standard GWR but probably of Mid Wales Railway origin.

Plate 12: Cwm Prysor, the windswept viaduct on the GWR Blaenau Festiniog branch, being traversed by the last train on 22nd January 1961. Regrettably, the weather did not stay fine for this notable event. The scenery on the line was superb.

Plate 13: Trawsfynydd sees the last train, on 22nd January 1961, hauled by two ex-GWR 0-6-0 pannier tanks sporting express passenger train headcodes. Strangely enough, Trawsfynydd still sees trains but it is served from the ex-LNWR branch from Llandudno Junction.

Plates 14 & 15: Scenes on the Wrexham to Ellesmere branch on 11th August 1962 *(above)* at Overton-on-Dee and *(below)* Bangor-on-Dee with an ex-GWR 0-4-2T 14XX class, No. 1432 and auto trailer with a single coach. The Wrexham to Ellesmere line closed to passengers on 10th September 1962. *(Below right)* Two Cambrian Railway labels, one for parcels and the other for passengers' luggage.

(880A) CAMBRIAN RAILWAYS. TO P,

Parcel

from MARCHWIEL

To _____

CAMBRIAN RAILWAY

TO

MARCHWIE

Plate 16: Llanidloes, on the Moat Lane Junction to Three Cocks Junction section known as the Mid Wales line, had a rather grandiose station building for the small amount of passengers that used it. Ivatt Class 2, 2-6-0, No. 46508 takes water whilst parcels are being loaded on 10th August 1962. The line closed to all traffic on 31st December 1962.

Plate 17: The Welshpool & Llanfair Railway closed to freight on 3rd November 1956 having closed to passengers on 9th February 1931. The line, of 2ft. 6in. gauge, was re-opened on 6th April 1963 and is happily still with us as a preserved railway running in the summer months. This photograph shows No. 822 *The Earl* on Banwy Viaduct on 23rd June 1956 with a special railtour. The viaduct over the River Banwy was severely damaged in a storm but was rebuilt by the army on behalf of the railway company.

Plate 18: A scene of tranquility graces Erwood on the Mid Wales line in August 1962. The line opened in 1864 and British Railways closed it in 1962. The station here appears unspoilt but devoid of passengers. Note the low platforms, the unusual layout and the staggered platforms.

Plate 19: Beyer Peacock 0-6-0, No. 822 of 1902 *The Earl* sizzles in the B R goods yard at Welshpool in the summer of 1956, prior to the closure of that line by British Railways in November 1956.

Plate 20: Presteign on 9th August 1962. The daily goods, with ex-GWR 14XX class, No. 1447 runs round its train. The passenger service ceased on 4th February 1951 and the line closed to freight on 28th September 1964.

G.W.R.

Presteign

Plate 21: Dolwen has, in this 1962 view, been demoted to an unstaffed halt. An Ivatt 2-6-0 runs in tender first with a Moat Lane to Llanidloes train. The service was withdrawn in December 1962.

Plate 22: Brecon was more of a centre for cross-country routes rather than a branch line terminal. Three now abandoned lengthy cross-country lines met here, the Neath & Brecon, the Brecon & Merthyr and the Midland line to Hereford, all of which had disappeared by 4th May 1964. This view was taken on 24th February 1962.

B.R.

(608.)

TO

BRECON

(B. & M.).

Plate 23: Pantydwr, with a leaky Ivatt Class 2, No. 46513 on a small pick-up freight in August 1962. The Ivatt Class 2-6-0 locomotive was always a very difficult engine to photograph as steam always seemed to leak out all over the place obscuring the subject, even in summer when the air was warm. The Ivatt Class 2s were first built by the LMS in 1946 but construction continued after nationalization.

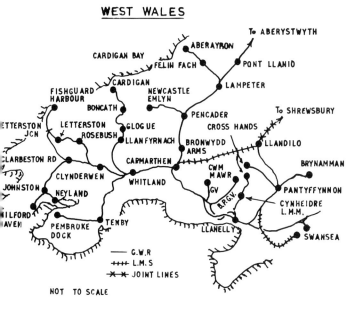

WEST WALES

WEST WALES

The South Wales Railway, built to Brunel's broad gauge, was opened from Swansea to Carmarthen in 1852 and extended to Neyland in 1856. The GWR absorbed the South Wales Railway in 1863 and the Pembroke & Tenby Railway was opened throughout to Whitland in 1866. The next line in the area to be constructed was the branch to Rosebush from Clynderwen. This line, the Meanclochog Railway, was opened for passengers on 19th September 1876, the extension from Meanclochog to Fishguard being opened on 1st July 1899 by the North Pembrokeshire & Fishguard Railway, thereby effecting a through route from the West Coast to the rest of England and Wales. The GWR, however, built its own more direct line, less severely graded, from Clarbeston Road to Letterston Junction and this was opened on 30th August 1906 when the new GWR Fishguard Harbour was opened. The North Pembrokeshire Railway was closed during World War I and the track was lifted and shipped to France. The line was not relaid until 1923. Passenger services were withdrawn on 25th October 1937 and freight, on 16th May 1949, from Clynderwen to Letterston. On 1st March 1965 Letterston to Letterston Junction closed to all traffic.

The 27½ mile long branch line from Whitland to Cardigan had a very slow passenger service. The passenger trains, of which there were four a day, took 1 hour 40 minutes to traverse the branch. Passenger services commenced throughout the line on 1st September 1886 and finished on 10th September 1962. Freight ceased on 27th May 1963. The nearby Newcastle Emlyn branch, not opened until 1st July 1895, was closed to passengers on 15th September 1952 and closed to all traffic on 1st October 1973. The Neyland branch closed to passengers on 15th June 1964.

The Aberayron to Lampeter line opened on 10th April 1911 and closed to passengers on 12th February 1951, having been absorbed by the GWR in 1923. The line was laid on flat bottom track and, after closure on 5th April 1965, the track was removed and some of it was re-used on the narrow gauge Vale of Rheidol line. The section from Felin Fach to Carmarthen did not close to all traffic until 1st October 1973. A preservation group, called the Gwili Railway, has re-opened a section of line at Bronwydd Arms on the Carmarthen to Pencader section. The main line north of Lampeter (Aberayron Junction) closed to all traffic on 22nd February 1965 as a result of flooding, except for the section from Pont Llanio to Lampeter which closed to freight on 1st October 1970.

Two minor standard gauge lines existed in West Glamorgan; the Burry Port & Gwendraeth Valley Railway, which is still open to Cwmmawr opencast site and the Llanelly & Mynydd Mawr Railway, which is also still in use as far as Cynheidre. The northern section of the branch to Cross Hands closed on 17th October 1966. Cwmmawr to Burry Port closed to passengers on 21st September 1953. These two coal-carrying concerns were grouped into the GWR in 1923 and now form part of the Western Region system. It is interesting to note that the Llanelly & Mynydd Mawr line did convey colliers, but not the general public, in their passenger trains. The workmen's service was operated in non-braked trains! The short branch to Mynydd-y-Garreg, of the former Gwendraeth Valley Railway, closed on 29th August 1960. The GWR Brynamman West branch closed to passengers on 18th August 1958 and to all traffic from Garnant. The rest of the line is still used by coal trains from Gwaun-cae-Gurwen.

Plate 24: Cardigan Station on 22nd May 1959 with the train from Whitland which comprises an ex-GWR 0-6-0 pannier tank, No. 1637 and one GWR corridor coach in BR red and cream livery. Note the lamp posts for the hanging of the oil lamps.

Plate 25: Pembroke Dock, 8th August 1962, with ex-G 2-6-2 tank, No. 4122 and GWR main line stock. Pembroke Dock branch is open for passenger traffic.

Plate 26: The Cardigan branch ran through sparsely-populated countryside over weed-covered tracks. Trains made lengthy stops at the intermediate stations en route. This view was photographed, at Glogue, on 22nd May 1959.

Plate 27: Llanfyrnach, with a Whitland to Cardigan train on 22nd May 1959. The line closed on 10th September 1962. Interesting pieces of architecture include the GWR corruagated iron huts on the platforms to store parcels and goods for collection off the train.

GLAMORGAN

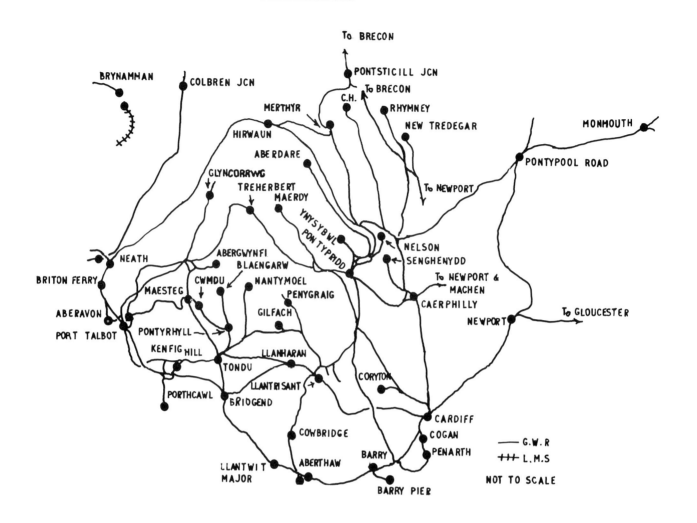

BRYNAMMAN   COLBREN JCN

To BRECON

PONTSTICILL JCN

To BRECON

C.H.   RHYMNEY

MERTHYR   NEW TREDEGAR

MONMOUTH

HIRWAUN

PONTYPOOL ROAD

ABERDARE

GLYNCORRWG

TREHERBERT

MAERDY

YNYSYBWL   To NEWPORT

PONTYPRIDD

NELSON   SENGHENYDD

NEATH

ABERGWYNFI   BLAENGARW

BRITON FERRY

CWMDU   NANTYMOEL

MAESTEG   PENYGRAIG

To NEWPORT & MACHEN

ABERAVON   GILFACH

PORT TALBOT   PONTYRHYLL

CAERPHILLY

NEWPORT

To GLOUCESTER

KENFIG HILL

LLANHARAN

TONDU

PORTHCAWL   LLANTRISANT

CORYTON

BRIDGEND

COWBRIDGE

CARDIFF   COGAN

BARRY   PENARTH

LLANTWIT MAJOR   ABERTHAW

——— G.W.R

+++ L.M.S

BARRY PIER

NOT TO SCALE

GWENT

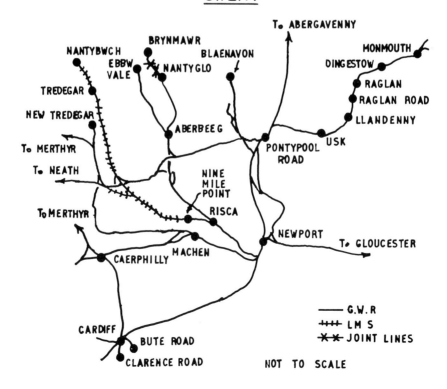

To ABERGAVENNY

NANTYBWCH   BRYNMAWR   BLAENAVON

MONMOUTH

EBBW VALE   NANTYGLO

DINGESTOW

TREDEGAR

RAGLAN

RAGLAN ROAD

NEW TREDEGAR

ABERBEEG

LLANDENNY

To MERTHYR

USK

To NEATH

PONTYPOOL ROAD

NINE MILE POINT

To MERTHYR

RISCA

CAERPHILLY   MACHEN

NEWPORT   To GLOUCESTER

——— G.W.R

+++ LM S

✕✕ JOINT LINES

CARDIFF   BUTE ROAD

CLARENCE ROAD

NOT TO SCALE

GLAMORGAN AND GWENT

A glance at the railway map of South Wales will reveal a multitude of lines running north to south down the valleys to the coast. Most of these lines were built in the nineteenth century and carried the high quality coal, mined in the area, down to the ports for shipment to overseas markets. With the running down of the coal industry, the rail network in the area has declined. Most of the valleys' lines could not be regarded as branch lines as they were really short distance mineral lines serving a specific industry. Some of these main lines did, however, have branches in the traditional sense.

Prior to the 1923 Grouping, the majority of the railways in South Wales were not owned by the Great Western Railway. The GWR acquired most of these by the Grouping in 1923. GWR lines in Glamorgan, prior to 1923, centred on the main line between Cardiff and Swansea and in the Bridgend and Llantrisant areas.

The GWR branch to Abergwynfi closed to passengers on 13th June 1960 having been opened in 1886; freight traffic ceasing at the end of 1969. Nearby, the Blaengarw and Nantymoel branches were traditional GWR branch lines worked by push-pull services usually comprising a pannier tank sandwiched in the middle of the train. The Blaengarw branch closed to passengers on 9th February 1953 and the Nantymoel branch on 5th May 1958. Both lines are still open for freight traffic. The Glyncorrwg branch, ex-South Wales Mineral Railway, ceased to function from 24th August 1970. The other GWR branch line in the area, to Penygraig, lost its passenger service on 9th June 1958 and its freight on 3rd April 1967. The short branch to Gilfach ceased to function on 5th June 1961. The GWR branch to the seaside town of Porthcawl closed to passengers on 9th September 1963 and to freight on 1st February 1965. The former Port Talbot Railway line, which joined the Blaengarw branch, closed on 9th May 1960, from Cwmdu and, on 31st August 1964, from Maesteg (Neath Road) to Port Talbot. The Port Talbot Railway (grouped with the GWR in 1923) passenger service from Port Talbot to Maesteg ceased on 11th September 1933 and services to Pontyrhyll ceased on 12th September 1932.

The Barry Railway operated in South Glamorgan and this highly successful concern paid high dividends to its shareholders during the great coal boom prior to World War I. The Barry Railway did not possess much in the way of branch lines but the rural cross-country line from Bridgend (the Vale of Glamorgan) passed off as the nearest thing that the Barry Railway had. Passenger services over this line ceased on 15th June 1964.

The Taff Vale Railway, the largest of the pre-group lines in South Wales, was another essentially coal-carrying railway but it did possess a few minor branch lines. The Taff Vale Railway owned a branch line to Aberthaw from Llantrisant. The line started out as the Cowbridge Railway and was opened in February 1865. The railway was extended as the Cowbridge & Aberthaw Railway and was opened on 1st October 1892. This became part of the Taff Vale Railway in 1895. Passenger services to Aberthaw ceased on 5th May 1930 and the line closed to freight on 1st November 1932. The Llantrisant to

Cowbridge section lost its passenger service on 26th November 1951. Freight ceased from Llantrisant to Llanharry on 28th July 1975 having ceased from there to Cowbridge on 1st February 1965. At the northern end of the system, the Maerdy branch closed to passengers on 15th June 1964 and the Aberdare (low level) line closed on 16th March 1964. Both lines are still open for freight although the Taff Vale and GWR branches to Aberdare have been swopped over at Cwmbach Junction enabling the Taff Vale trackbed into Aberdare to be used by the local authority for road improvement schemes. Another Taff Vale branch closed in the area was that to Ynysybwl which closed to passengers on 28th July 1952 and to freight on 2nd November 1959. The Pontypridd to Llantrisant passenger trains finished on 31st March 1952. The Taff Vale also had a short branch to Nelson which closed to passengers on 12th September 1932.

The Rhymney Railway, a great rival of the Taff Vale, did have a traditional branch line to Senghenydd, referred to as the Aber branch, and was opened on 1st February 1894. The line was one of the Rhymney Railway branch lines to be worked by a steam railcar at the turn of the century and was closed to all traffic on 15th June 1964.

The Brecon & Merthyr Railway had two branch lines straying off from its long winding main line from Newport to Brecon. One of these was a line to Rhymney (up the other side of the valley from the railway of that name), closed to all traffic from Rhymney to Tredegar on 14th April 1930, and then from New Tredegar to Aberbargoed Junction on 31st December 1962. The other line was more of a traditional GWR branch line worked by railmotors and with rail level halts. The Machen to Caerphilly branch was unique in that the 'up' and 'down' lines ran on separate alignments and had intermediate halts on each separate line, so that one halt gave a service in one direction only and another, on the other side of the Rhymney River, served only trains travelling in the opposite direction. This curious line lost its passenger service on 17th September 1956, with freight ceasing on 20th July 1964 ('up' line) and on 20th November 1967 ('down' line). The Brecon & Merthyr Railway was unique in that the railway was in two separate sections, the connection between the two being bridged by 2¾ miles of the Rhymney Railway from Bargoed to Deri Junction. Another peculiarity in Glamorgan, is the line from Coryton, still open and worked as a branch line from Cardiff. This was, however, once the main line of the Cardiff Railway but was cut back, on 16th June 1952, from Pontypridd.

In Gwent, the Western Region valley lines from Blaenavon, Brynmawr and Ebbw Vale closed to passengers on 30th April 1962. The Pontypool Road to Monmouth branch closed to passengers from 13th June 1955, the section from Usk to Monmouth being closed to all traffic. Glascoed to Usk closed to freight on 13th September 1965. The last passenger train was a special, organized by the Stephenson Locomotive Society, which ran on 12th October 1957. Monmouth to Lydbrook Junction closed to all traffic on 5th January 1959.

Plate 28: Aberbeeg, showing the junction for the Ebbw Vale and Brynmawr branches on 7th April 1962 by which time the lines had been dieselized. On the left can be seen a fine GWR all wood bracket signal which is oil-lit, while the station buildings are gas-lit. These lines closed to passengers on 30th April 1962.

Plate 29: Ebbw Vale, the GWR branch terminus, on 7th April 1962, with the early morning newspapers and parcels train which was worked by an ex-GWR 0-6-0 pannier tank. The line closed to passengers on 30th April 1962.

Plate 30: Express passenger work for a pannier tank; well here is the proof! The 94XX class 0-6-0PT, No. 9468 is sporting an express passenger train headcode as it bowls through Cogan on 3rd July 1960 with a Newport to Barry excursion. The 94XX class was rated as Class 4 by the BRB and was introduced by the GWR in 1947.

Plate 31: Aberbeeg was the junction for the Ebbw Vale and Brynmawr branches which were dieselized in 1958 just four years before withdrawal of the passenger services, which took place on 30th April 1962.

Taff Vale Railway

PONTYPRIDD

TO

COWBRIDGE

Plate 32:   Clarence Road on 24th February 1962. This was a small single platform terminus at Cardiff, near the docks, which closed on 16th March 1964.

B.R.

(608.)

TO

CLARENCE RD.

(G. W. R.).

Plate 33: Blaenavon, on 2nd Apr. 1962, with a diesel multiple unit in B.R. green livery with the yellow flash on it front. Blaenavon (low level) was th GWR terminus which closed to passen gers on 30th April 1962. The high leve station was on the former LNWR branc which closed to all traffic on 24th Jun 1954.

Plate 34:   Pontsticill Junction, with ex-GWR pannier tank, No. 7736 on a Brecon to Newport train on 24th February 1962. Pontsticill Junction was the point where the Merthyr line left the former Brecon & Merthyr main line from Newport. The Brecon & Merthyr Railway had the distinction of having a break of 2¾ miles in its system, where trains had to run over the Rhymney Railway from Bargoed to Deri Junction. The line closed to passengers on 31st December 1962.

Plate 35:   Senghenydd, seen on 16th April 1960 with a diesel multiple unit, was a branch line of the former Rhymney Railway and closed to all traffic on 15th June 1964.

Plate 36: Bridgend, on 4th January 1958, with ex-GWR 'Hall' class, No. 5990 *Dorford Hall* chugging out on a stopping passenger service to Swansea. The station nameboard refers to the Llynvi & Ogmore branches and the Vale of Glamorgan Railway, the former names of branch lines which joined the main line at Bridgend.

Plate 37: Porthcawl, on 7th August 1962; a seaside terminus in South Wales which closed to passengers on 9th September 1963 and to freight on 1st February 1965. The train is of interest here as it is being worked as an auto train (push-pull) with the locomotive, an ex-GWR pannier tank, sandwiched in the centre. This made, in effect, a multiple unit steam train!

Plate 38: A Class 4, 2-6-4 tank blasts away at Pantyffynnon, with a Central Wales train for Swansea, on 15th June 1963. On the right is the branch train for Brynamman composed of ex-GWR rolling stock.

te 39: Brynamman West, with
few passengers waiting for the
in from Pantyffynnon on 9th
gust 1958. The line closed on
th August 1958 to all traffic
m Garnant.

Plates 40 to 42: The last train from Pontypool Road to Monmouth on 12 October 1957 hauled by ex-GWR 0-6-0 pannier tank, No. 4668. The line had closed to regular traffic two years earlier. (Left) The special at Dingestow and GWR pine trees specially planted when the line was opened. (Centre) Closing the gates at Llandenny en route to Monmouth, and (bottom) the return from Monmouth showing the overgrown Raglan Road Crossing Halt.

G.W.R.

(W. & S. Ltd.)

MONMOUTH

(MAY HILL)

G.W.R.

Monmouth

TROY

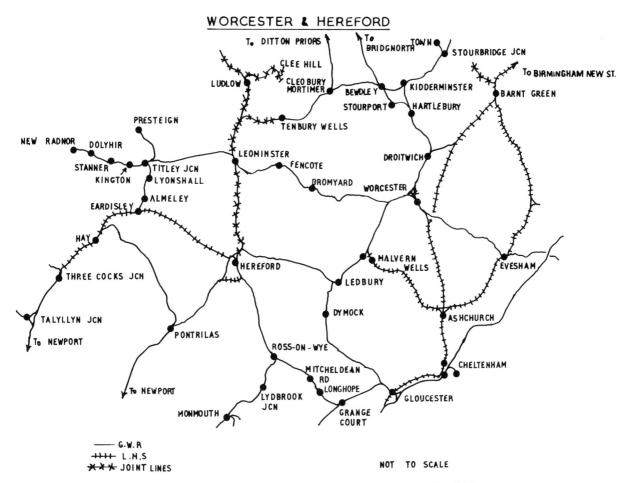

Legend:
— G.W.R
+++ L.N.S
✕✕✕ JOINT LINES

NOT TO SCALE

WORCESTERSHIRE AND HEREFORDSHIRE

In West Herefordshire, the railway system based on Kington started out as a narrow gauge 3 ft. 6 in. line called the Kington Railway which opened in 1820. The first standard gauge line to Kington was opened from Leominster in 1857. The Kington Railway was converted to standard gauge and the New Radnor and Presteign branches opened in 1875.

The New Radnor and Presteign branches lost their passenger services on 5th February 1951. The passenger service from Kington to Leominster was withdrawn on 7th February 1955. Freight services from New Radnor to Dolyhir ceased on 31st December 1951 and from Dolyhir to Kington on 9th June 1958. All traffic from Presteign and Kington to Leominster ceased on 28th September 1964.

The Kington Railway, from Eardisley to Titley, closed on 1st July 1940 to all traffic. The Golden Valley line from Hay to Pontrilas closed on 15th December 1941 to all traffic, except on the section from Abbeydore to Pontrilas which closed to freight on 3rd June 1957. The short section from Pontrilas to Moss ceased to function on 31st March 1969.

The last train from Leominster to Bromyard ran on 26th April 1958 hauled by ex-GWR 45XX class 2-6-2T No. 4571, regular trains, both passenger and freight, having ceased on 15th September 1952. Therefore, the last train ran six years after the line had closed: quite a record! The Bromyard to Worcester section lasted longer and closed to all traffic, from Bromyard to Bransford Road Junction, on 7th September 1964.

The Tenbury Wells to Woofferton service, over GW & LMS Joint lines, ceased on 31st July 1961 to all traffic. The Tenbury Wells to Cleobury Mortimer line closed on 6th January 1964 to all traffic, the passenger service, through to Bewdley, having finished on 1st August 1962. The freight traffic from Cleobury Mortimer to Bewdley ceased on 16th April 1965 at the same time as the Ditton Priors branch which had lost its passenger service on 26th September 1938. The Cleobury Mortimer & Ditton Priors Light Railway was independent until 1923 but was taken over by the GWR. The line was notable for the use of GWR pannier tanks with American-style balloon stack chimneys used to prevent sparks scattering in the Admiralty sidings where munitions were stored. The Bewdley to Hartlebury and Kidderminster line closed to passengers on 5th January 1970, the Severn Valley line to Shrewsbury having lost its passenger trains on 9th September 1963. Stourport-on-Severn to Bewdley also closed to freight on 5th January 1970. The Severn Valley line now runs from Bewdley to Bridgnorth and connecting services are now provided from Kidderminster to Bewdley in the summer to serve the Severn Valley Railway, a GWR branch which has been restored. The stations on the Severn Valley line have also been lovingly restored to their original GWR colours.

The Stourbridge Town branch is still open for passenger traffic, worked by single unit railcars. Hereford to Grange Court closed to passengers on 2nd November 1964, the Monmouth to Ross-on-Wye line closing to passengers on 5th January 1959. The freight service from Lydbrook to Grange Court, via Ross-on-Wye, ended on 1st November 1965. Hereford to Ross-on-Wye closed to all traffic on 2nd November 1964. There were two routes from Hereford to Gloucester, one being via Ross-on-Wye, the other via Ledbury. The Gloucester and Ledbury branch was worked by GWR railcars. These were single unit vehicles introduced by the GWR in the 1930s. This passenger service ceased on 13th July 1959, Dymock to Ledbury closing to all traffic on this date. Dymock to Gloucester (Over Junction) closed to freight traffic on 15th June 1964.

Plate 43: The last train from Bromyard to Leominster, an SLS special, on 26th April 1958, is about to leave Bromyard. Passenger services were withdrawn on 15th September 1952.

Plate 44: An ex-GWR 41XX class, No. 4107 takes water at Longhope on the Hereford to Gloucester branch on 4th April 1964. In this picture the stands for receiving the single line tablet can be seen, with the lamps for night use, at the end of the platform. Several examples of the GWR large 2-6-2 passenger tank exist on the preserved railways, the Severn Valley Railway having three which is ideal for a line of that length.

Plates 45 & 46: The Kington goods hauled by ex-GWR 14XX class 0-4-2 tank, No. 1447, on 9th August 1962. *(Below)* The train stops at Titley Junction and *(above)* sits in the platform at Kington, the station signs still being intact although passenger services terminated in 1955. The freight service ceased on 28th September 1964.

G. W. R.

KINGTON

Plate 47: Lyonshall, or its remains, on the Kington to Eardisley section as it was on 27th April 1963. The line closed to all traffic on 1st July 1940 and the rails were used elsewhere. The line was formerly the Kington Railway opened in 1820 and built to a gauge of 3 ft. 6 in. In this view, the road bridge has been taken out cutting the station in half.

Plate 48: Tenbury Wells on 12th September 1959 showing an ex-GWR 14XX class 0-4-2T on the auto train to Ludlow over the former GW & LNWR Joint line. The station was built on the site of the wharf of the Leominster Canal. The line to Woofferton closed on 31st July 1961 whilst the line to Bewdley closed, to all traffic, on 6th January 1964. Passenger services to Bewdley were withdrawn on 1st August 1962.

G.W.R.

CLEOBURY MORTIM

G.W.R.

NEEN SOLLAR

Plate 49: Ledbury was a country junction on the Worcester to Hereford line for the Ledbury to Gloucester branch. Ex-GWR 'Hall' class, No. 5990 *Dorford Hall* steams in from Worcester on 23rd August 1958. The branch train would then follow on behind once the main line was clear. In this scene are GWR signals, lamps, platform trolley, seats and even a few passengers! The passenger service over the branch to Gloucester ceased on 13th July 1959.

Plate 50: Ross-on-Wye, on 4th April 1964, with a dirty ex-GWR Mogul, No. 6346 on a Hereford to Gloucester train. Note the freight avoiding line which runs round behind the station.

Plate 51: Mitcheldean Road with an ex-GWR 2-6-2 tank, No. 4161 on a Gloucester to Hereford train, on 4th April 1964. Note how the platform edges have been eaten away by frost during the winter. The passenger service was withdrawn on 2nd November 1964, the line closing to all traffic from Hereford to Ross-on-Wye. The line on to Gloucester, via Grange Court, closed to freight on 1st November 1965.

Plate 52: A relic of the Ross-on-Wye to Monmouth branch which was worked by an auto train where the guard issued the tickets. This practice was widely adopted by the GWR and Western Region. The intermediate stations and halts were unstaffed on many branch lines and the 'bell punch' tickets were issued on the train similar to those issued on the buses.

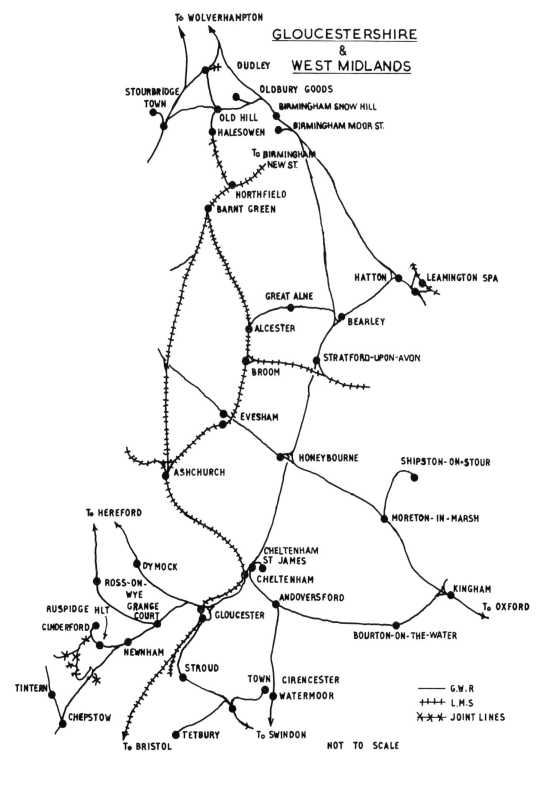

GLOUCESTERSHIRE AND THE WEST MIDLANDS

Two traditional GWR branch lines existed in South Gloucestershire, one to Tetbury and the other to Cirencester Town and both were worked by GWR 0-4-2 passenger tank and push-pull stock. These eventually became replaced, in 1959, by four-wheeled railbuses of English or German origin. These were similar to the Deutsche Bundesbahn railbuses which are still to be seen trundling around on the German minor lines. The passenger services were withdrawn, on 6th April 1964, on the Cirencester Town branch as were all services on the Tetbury branch. Freight services to Cirencester Town terminated on 4th October 1965. The former cross-country Midland & South Western Junction Railway from Cheltenham to Swindon via Cirencester closed to all traffic on 11th September 1961 from Andoversford to Cirencester Watermoor. The trackbed through Cirencester now forms part of the town bypass whilst the Cirencester Town Station now has a new lease of life as the local bus station.

The Cheltenham to Kingham branch closed to passengers on 15th October 1962, to freight from Bourton-on-the-Water to Kingham on 7th September 1964, and to freight from Cheltenham to Bourton on 15th October 1962.

The Moreton-in-Marsh to Shipston-on-Stour branch closed to passengers as early as 8th June 1929 having been built over part of the Stratford Tramway, a 4 ft. gauge tramway which opened in 1825. The freight services on this line were withdrawn from 2nd May 1960.

The saga of the Bearley to Alcester line is as follows. Regular passenger services ceased on 25th September 1939, but after Coventry was bombed out in November 1940, a workmen's service was introduced to Great Alne from Leamington and continued until 3rd July 1944. The freight service ceased on the line from 1st March 1951 and the line was then used to store redundant wagons. The connection from Bearley North Junction to the Alcester branch was removed on 28th August 1960. The cross-country line from Cheltenham Spa to Stratford-upon-Avon ceased to carry passengers from 25th March 1968. The short Cheltenham St. James branch closed on 3rd January 1966 to passengers and on 1st June 1966 to freight.

To the south-west of Gloucester the Chepstow to Monmouth line, along the Wye Valley, lost its passenger service on 5th January 1959 and freight traffic was discontinued between Tintern and Monmouth Troy on 6th January 1964. In the Forest of Dean, the Great Western branch to Cinderford from Newnham closed to passengers on 3rd November 1958 and to freight on 1st August 1967. Grange Court to Ross-on-Wye closed on 1st November 1965 to freight traffic, having closed to passengers on 2nd November 1964. The Gloucester to Ledbury branch, worked by the GWR railcars introduced during the 1930s, closed to passengers on 13th July 1959, freight services lasting to Dymock until 15th June 1964.

In the Black Country, the Halesowen to Old Hill branch succumbed to bus competition as early as 5th December 1927 and closed to freight on 1st October 1969. The Old Hill to Dudley line, which had a GWR push-pull service, closed to passengers on 15th June 1964, and to freight on 1st January 1968. The short goods branch to Oldbury closed on 7th September 1964. Stourbridge Town and Moor Street are still open, if somewhat altered from their original appearance.

Plate 53: Ex-GWR 14XX class, No. 1472 whistles up for Kemble on the last train from Tetbury on 5th April 1964.

Plate 54: The last day at Tetbury with ex-GWR 0-4-2T, No. 1472 on 5th April 1964. The line was usually worked by rail-buses but, on the occasion of the last day, steam power was utilized. The GWR 14XX class locomotives were built between 1931 and 1936 and totalled 95, four of which survive today.

Plate 55: Tetbury, seen in its ...tter years, photographed on ...d July 1960. The station ...mps, lit by gas, are of GWR ...igin and the setting, complete ...th conifers, seems cosy if not ...cturesque. Regrettably, the ...e has now been obliterated.

Plate 56: Bourton-on-the-Water, a Cotswold line, with an ex-GWR 41XX class 2-6-2 side tank running bunker first on 26th April 1958. The GWR rebuilt Bourton Station in the 1930s in a Cotswold style using stone and heavy timberwork. The branch from Kingham to Cheltenham closed to passengers on 15th October 1962. Freight traffic was discontinued on 7th September 1964 between Bourton-on-the-Water and Kingham, having been discontinued between Cheltenham and Bourton on 15th October 1962.

Plate 57: Old Hill, on 17th March 1962, showing an ex-GWR 41XX class 2-6-2 side tank arriving with a Birmingham (Snow Hill) to Stourbridge stopping train. The photograph is, in fact, taken from the Halesowen branch platform, or site thereof. The Halesowen branch finished on 1st October 1969. At the end of the platform a standard GWR water tower, of the cylindrical type, can be seen.

tes 58 & 59: Shipston-on-Stour closed to freight from 2nd May 1960 as own in the notice. The goods from Moreton-in-Marsh ran twice weekly and s hauled by a BR Standard Class 2, 2-6-2, in this case No. 78008. *(Above)* e freight can be seen, on 19th April 1960, near Stretton-on-Fosse and *elow)* at Longdon Road where the former Stratford Tramway diverged to ratford-upon-Avon. The Shipston-on-Stour branch closed to passengers on h July 1929.

SHROPSHIRE

Shrewsbury was a great railway centre and the terminus of the one time Shropshire & Montgomery Railway which, although not incorporated into the GWR, came into its successor, the Western Region. The military who took the line over during the war, handed the line back to British Railways but the line last saw a train in 1960. The GWR had access to Crewe via Wellington and Market Drayton. This was a long cross-country line which local people used and had small halts which were built by the GWR in the inter-war years. The passenger travelling from Wellington to Nantwich passed such delightfully-named places as Crudgington, Ellerdine Halt, Peplow, Hodnet, Tern Hill, Audlem and Coole Pilate Halt. These picturesque country halts closed on 9th September 1963. Freight traffic lasted until 1st May 1967.

The Severn Valley line from Bewdley to Shrewsbury closed to all traffic on 2nd December 1963 from Shrewsbury (Sutton Bridge Junction) to Alveley. Alveley Sidings to Bewdley closed to freight on 3rd February 1969. The Severn Valley Railway started operations from Bridgnorth to Highley in April 1974 as a preserved line and has not looked back since.

The Longville branch closed to all traffic on 2nd December 1963 from Buildwas to Longville. Freight services from Longville through to Craven Arms, on the Shrewsbury & Hereford Joint line, were discontinued on 31st December 1951 at the same time that passenger services were withdrawn throughout from Craven Arms to Much Wenlock. Much Wenlock to Wellington closed to passengers on 23rd July 1962. The section from Horsehay to Ketley Junction closed to all traffic on 6th July 1964. The Buildwas to Madeley Junction section did have a passenger service until 1915, but this line has now had a new lease of life as far as passengers are concerned. In addition to the regular merry-go-round coal and oil trains to Ironbridge Power-Station, a passenger service was re-introduced in May 1979 to a new station named Telford (Coalbrookdale), a station built to serve the museum and historic relics at Ironbridge. A passenger service now runs on summer Sundays from Birmingham New Street to the new station. In the south of Shropshire, the Ditton Priors branch closed to passengers on 26th September 1938, and to freight on 16th April 1965.

SHROPSHIRE

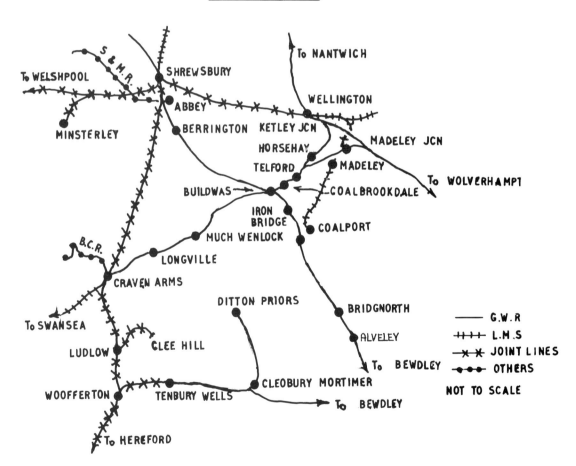

G.W.R.

Ironbridge
AND
Broseley

G. W. R.

Berrington
(S.V.)

ate 60: Ludlow, on the Shrewsbury & Hereford Joint line sees ex-GWR 0-4-2T, No. *55 about to set off backwards to Woofferton and Tenbury Wells. These locomotives *ways looked very old but were, in fact, built by the GWR at Swindon between 1932 *d 1936. The 95 locomotives in the 14XX class were built for branch line work, *lacing a much older class of 0-4-2 tank dating from the nineteenth century.

te 61: Berrington, on the Severn Valley line; a station no longer open. The northern *lf of the line closed to all traffic on 2nd December 1963 from Shrewsbury to Alveley *dings. This photograph was taken on 9th April 1960 and shows the 'prize' length of *ck. Each year, every engineer's district entered the best kept length of track competi-*n for which a prize was awarded, to the gang responsible, by the Chief Permanent Way *gineer. Lengths of track in less busy areas, where there was less wear and tear, stood a *tter chance of winning!

Plate 62: Longville, on 28th April 1963, when the line was still open to the occasional goods train. The freight traffic ceased to run on 2nd December 1963 from Buildwas. The passenger service over this line ceased on 31st December 1951.

Plate 63: A picturesque view Much Wenlock on 28th Ap 1963. Passenger services fro Much Wenlock to Wellingt finished the previous year, 23rd July 1962. The freig services ceased, from Longvi to Buildwas, on 2nd Decem 1963.

Plate 64:   A quiet moment at Wellington, whilst the ex-GWR 41XX class 2-6-2T uncouples from the 7.00 a.m. from Crewe on 21st September 1958.

OXFORDSHIRE

The 'Old Worse and Worse', as the Oxford to Worcester line was known, left the GWR at Wolvercote Junction and headed west through the Cotswolds. The Oxford, Worcester & Wolverhampton Railway was taken over by the GWR and formed part of that system. In 1863, the GWR took over the West Midland Railway which had incorporated the OWWR. The OWWR main line had a short undulating branch from Moreton-in-Marsh to Shipston-on-Stour, but this line was built partly over the Stratford Tramway (a horse-worked concern which was closed during World War I) and closed to passengers as early as 1929. The Stratford Tramway was lifted to provide metal for the war effort. Freight traffic to Shipston-on-Stour ceased on 2nd May 1960.

An important country junction, on the main line from Oxford to Worcester, was that at Kingham which had trains to Chipping Norton and Banbury in the easterly direction and to Cheltenham in the west. Kingham to Chipping Norton closed to passengers on 12th December 1962, the service through to Banbury having been withdrawn on 4th July 1951. The freight service from Kingham to Chipping Norton was withdrawn on 7th September 1964. The freight service from Chipping Norton to Great Rollright ceased on 3rd December 1962, the same day as the passenger service from Kingham to Chipping Norton ceased, the service through to Hook Norton from Great Rollright having been withdrawn in September 1958. Adderbury to Hook Norton closed to freight on 4th November 1963 and Adderbury to King's Sutton on 18th

August 1969. The line westwards from Kingham to Cheltenham closed to passengers on 15th October 1962, closing to all traffic from Cheltenham to Bourton-on-the-Water on the same day. The freight to Kingham, from Bourton-on-the-Water lasted until 7th September 1964, the same day as from Chipping Norton.

A great favourite with visitors was the lengthy branch from Oxford to Fairford, which closed to passengers on 18th June 1962. All traffic from Witney to Fairford ceased at the same time. The Witney branch lasted until 2nd November 1970 for freight traffic. Little remains of the Witney and Fairford line today, the terminus of Fairford having been obliterated. The station buildings do remain at Eynsham and these were painted green and cream, an experimental GWR livery which was not adopted. The faded green paintwork can still be seen. The short Blenheim & Woodstock branch nearby closed completely on 1st March 1954.

The shortest route to Oxford from London was via Princes Risborough and Thame, a route shorter by 7¾ miles than the main line via Didcot. The passenger service from Princes Risborough to Oxford was withdrawn on 7th January 1963, the section from Thame to Morris Cowley closing to all traffic on 1st May 1967. The Princes Risborough to Watlington branch closed to all traffic from Chinnor to Watlington on 2nd January 1961, the passenger service over the whole branch having ceased on 1st July 1957.

OXFORDSHIRE

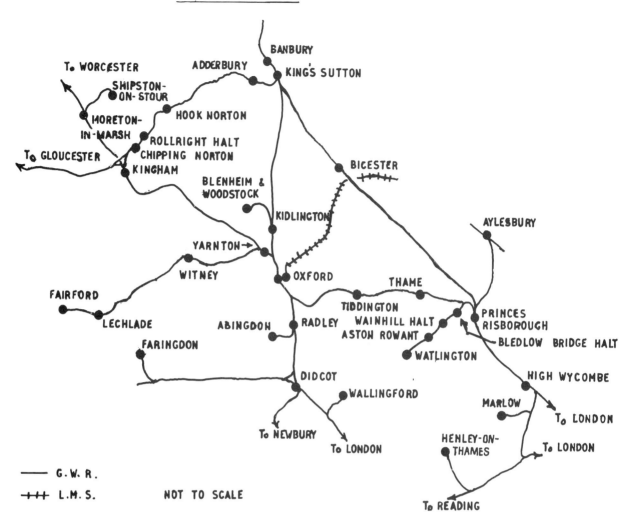

To WORCESTER
SHIPSTON-ON-STOUR
ADDERBURY
BANBURY
KING'S SUTTON
MORETON-IN-MARSH
HOOK NORTON
ROLLRIGHT HALT
CHIPPING NORTON
To GLOUCESTER
KINGHAM
BLENHEIM & WOODSTOCK
BICESTER
KIDLINGTON
AYLESBURY
YARNTON
WITNEY
OXFORD
THAME
FAIRFORD
TIDDINGTON
PRINCES RISBOROUGH
LECHLADE
ABINGDON
RADLEY
WAINHILL HALT
ASTON ROWANT
BLEDLOW BRIDGE HALT
FARINGDON
WATLINGTON
HIGH WYCOMBE
DIDCOT
WALLINGFORD
MARLOW
To LONDON
To NEWBURY
To LONDON
HENLEY-ON-THAMES
To LONDON
To READING

——— G.W.R.
+++ L.M.S.   NOT TO SCALE

Plate 66: Ex-GWR pannier tank, No. 3697 runs round at Watlington in the pouring rain, on 9th March 1957.

◀ *Plate 65 (left):* The short single platform at Watlington, on 9th March 1957, as seen from an adjoining field. The station building is still there, complete with goods shed and corrugated iron huts (for oil lamps), but today the whole scene is very overgrown with, of course, no track.

Plate 67: Thame, with its famous overall roof, photographed on 20th July 1958. The station still exists, but without the commodious buildings, as the line is used by oil trains to an unloading terminal at Thame.

Plate 68: An ex-GWR 61XX 2-6-2 tank pauses at Tiddington with an Oxford to Princes Risborough stopping train on 20th March 1962. The branch closed to passengers on 7th January 1963.

Plate 69: An ex-GWR 14XX class 0-4-2T arrives at Lechlade on 10th February 1962. There is little evidence of this station now as the buildings have been demolished. This GWR country station depicted with its bicycle shed, signal box, with horseshoe over the door, and station garden opposite the platform is, alas, no more. The line closed to all traffic on this section of the line on 18th June 1962.

Plate 70: The scene at Witney, on the Fairford branch, on 10th February 1962 with an ex-GWR 0-6-0 pannier tank moving up the platform to take water from the column at the end of the platform. The station lamps, of GWR design, have shades on them; possibly a wartime addition. The passenger service finished on 18th June 1962 and Witney, as a goods only branch, closed on 2nd November 1970.

Plate 71:   The East Gloucestershire terminus of Fairford, as seen from the road overbridge, on 10th February 1962. The ex-GWR locomotive, No. 1468 has turned and taken water after having worked the train in from Oxford. The engine shed at Fairford was some ½ mile beyond the station. The line closed on 18th June 1962.

Plate 72:   The last train about to leave Chipping Norton on 1st December 1962. Detonators are being placed on the track in front of locomotive No. 78001, a BR Class 2, 2-6-2. This was common practice at closures. Photography was difficult, to say the least, as it was December, almost dark and freezing cold. *(Right)* The ticket issued for the last train.

Plates 73 to 76: Scenes on the Watlington branch on 26th June 1957, the last day of passenger operations. *(Top left)* A view of Bledlow Bridge Halt, from the leading railmotor, showing the rail level platform and oil lamp, complete with step. *(Top right)* Another passenger's view of Wainhill Halt with the crossing keeper about to shut the gate, and *(below)* Chinnor Station, one of only two intermediate complete stations on the branch. *(Bottom right)* The Western Region closure notice for the branch.

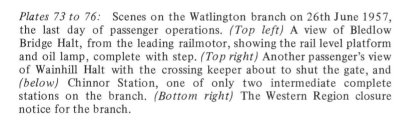

BRITISH RAILWAYS (WESTERN REGION)

PUBLIC NOTICE

THE BRITISH TRANSPORT COMMISSION HEREBY GIVE NOTICE THAT ON AND FROM MONDAY, 1ST JULY, 1957, THE PASSENGER TRAIN SERVICE WILL BE WITHDRAWN BETWEEN PRINCES RISBOROUGH AND WATLINGTON, AND A PASSENGER ROAD SERVICE WILL BE PROVIDED BY THE CITY OF OXFORD MOTOR SERVICES LTD.

THE COLLECTION AND DELIVERY ARRANGEMENTS FOR PARCELS TRAFFIC WILL REMAIN UNDISTURBED.

ANY FURTHER INFORMATION REQUIRED CAN BE OBTAINED UPON APPLICATION TO THE STATION MASTER OR MR. N.H.BRIANT, DISTRICT OPERATING SUPERINTENDENT, PADDINGTON STATION, W.2.

PADDINGTON STATION
MAY, 1957

K.W.C.GRAND
GENERAL MANAGER

Plates 77 to 79: More relics of the Watlington branch. *(Above)* The
goods shed at Aston Rowant, with an approaching auto train, on 9th
March 1957. *(Below)* The last day, 29th June 1957, with ex-GWR
pannier tank, No. 4650, auto train, and goods shed. *(Right)* Travel
to Watlington, in 1957, included an LNER single from Marylebone,
a GWR return from Princes Risborough and a printed return from
Paddington, price 3/4½d (17p)!. A GWR parcels label to Paddington
is also included.

LONDON AREA

The Great Western in the London area did not have much of a suburban network unlike most of the other companies. The GWR only had one main line westwards from Paddington (opened in 1838) until the turn of the century. When the Great Central Railway arrived on the scene, the GWR built a new cut-off line from Old Oak Junction through Greenford and Denham to join up with the former GWR Aylesbury branch, which ran through High Wycombe and Princes Risborough. The GWR also built a new line from Princes Risborough to join up with the old main line, north of Oxford, at Aynho Junction near King's Sutton. These new works and cut-offs (1903–1910) were a feature of GWR expansion at the turn of the century and made the journey to the West Midlands and Birmingham much easier than the old 'Great Way Round', via Oxford. The Aylesbury branch was opened in 1863 as a broad gauge line from Maidenhead, running through High Wycombe and Princes Risborough. When the Great Central line was built, the Princes Risborough to Aylesbury section became a jointly-owned branch line and is still open. The section from High Wycombe to Bourne End closed on 4th May 1970 to all traffic. Marlow to Bourne End is another surviving line being served from Maidenhead by

single unit railcars replacing the former GWR railmotors worked by 14XX class 0-4-2 tanks. The Henley-on-Thames and Windsor & Eton branches are also still open although desecrated by rationalization. Windsor & Eton is claimed to be the biggest unstaffed halt on the region!

Uxbridge was well-endowed with railways and, in addition to the Metropolitan and Piccadilly lines of London Transport, had two short GWR branch lines. The northern branch, to High Street, was worked by an 0-4-2 tank and push-pull stock from Denham on the main line. The Uxbridge High Street line lost its passenger service on 1st September 1939, the Vine Street line closing to passengers on 10th September 1962. Freight services were withdrawn from both lines on 24th February 1964. The Greenford to Ealing Broadway service is still in operation, diesel multiple units having replaced the GWR push-pull units operated by 14XX class 0-4-2 tanks. The Staines West branch, formerly operated by GWR single unit railcars, closed to passengers on 29th March 1965. The Brentford branch is also still in use for goods traffic, the passenger service having been withdrawn on 4th May 1942, the extension from Brentford Town to Brentford Dock having closed to freight on 31st December 1964.

LONDON AREA

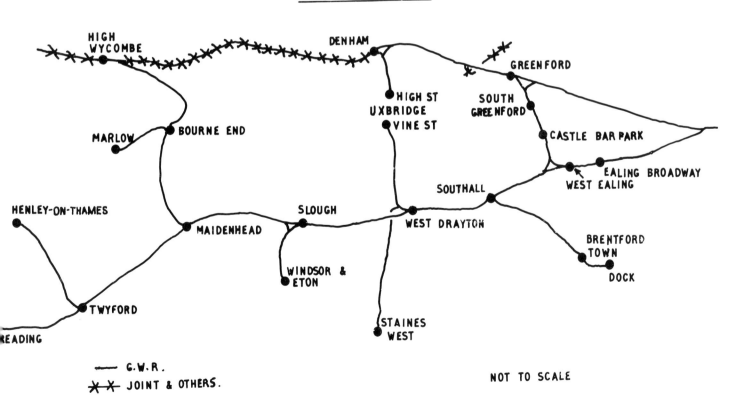

Plate 80: Ex-GWR 'Castle' class, No. 7022 *Hereford Castle* has strayed off the main line in this February 1958 photograph, taken on the Greenford to Ealing branch. The normal push-pull service had been withdrawn on this day owing to engineering works. The 'Castle' is hauling BR Mk I stock in chocolate and cream livery.

Plate 81: Ex-GWR 'Modifi Hall', No. 7926 *Willey Hall* se on the Greenford to Ealing li with the 1.20 p.m. Paddington Weymouth train, on 16 February 1958. The chocola and cream coaches include o of GWR origin.

Plates 82 & 83: Scenes on the Greenford to Ealing branch showing *(above)* ex-GWR 61XX class 2-6-2T, No. 6156 at Castle Bar Park Halt heading a stopping train from Paddington to Reading, on 16th February 1958. *(Below)* A locomotive of the same class works bunker first through South Greenford Halt on 2nd March 1958. This was a very good example of a GWR 'pagoda' structure halt opened between the wars. The halt was opened on 20th September 1926.

Plate 84: The 'Marlow Donkey' at rest with ex-GWR 0-4-2T, No 1421 at the head on 5th March 1961. All the platform furniture is in evidence; trolleys, parcels, gas lamps with black-out shades and even the cattle dock is usable as well as the goods yard. A visit today to the still open station reveals a solitary platform, no sidings and an absence of staff.

Plate 85: Interesting GWR shunt signals adorn the end of the platform at West Drayton on the main line and junction for the Staines and Uxbridge branches. The signals with the holes were a GWR peculiarity not installed after 1949 and were known as 'twin-armed backing signals', presumably used so that a train could back into the sidings out of the platform after having arrived off one of the branches. *(Below)* Ticket and luggage label relics from closed suburban stations.

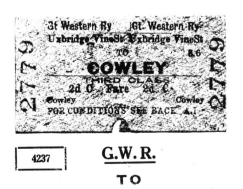

WILTSHIRE AND BERKSHIRE

In Wiltshire, the short branch from Malmesbury to Little Somerford closed to passengers on 10th September 1951, Little Somerford being on another GWR cut-off line built from Wootton Bassett to Badminton in 1903. The Malmesbury branch formerly joined up with the Chippenham line at Dauntsey, the Dauntesey to Somerford line having closed on 17th July 1933. Freight traffic ceased between Little Somerford and Malmesbury on 12th November 1962. The Chippenham to Calne line closed on 20th September 1965 and the cross-country line from Holt Junction to Patney & Churton, through Devizes, closed on 18th April 1966, both lines to all traffic. The Trowbridge to Thingley Junction line to Chippenham still sees the occasional passenger train and engineer's diversions at weekends. The former Midland & South Western Junction Railway, running from Cheltenham to the Southern main line at Andover Junction, had a tiny branch line from Ludgershall to Tidworth. This line was used mainly by military traffic and closed to passenger traffic on 19th September 1955. The military took the line over during 1955 and eventually closed it to freight on 31st July 1963. The Midland & South Western Junction Railway was absorbed by the GWR at the Grouping in 1923. This accounted for the curious situation with two lines serving Marlborough as the GWR served Marlborough with a branch from Savernake whilst the MSWJ went sailing through to Andover on its own tracks. The GWR station at Marlborough closed on 6th March 1933, all trains being diverted to the former MSWJ station. The Great Western had a works train service which operated from Swindon to Highworth and as the train was not advertised to the public, it was possible to have a free ride on the branch. The Highworth branch closed to regular passenger trains on 2nd March 1953 but the workmen's trains ran until 6th August 1962 after which date the line was abandoned. The short Faringdon to Uffington branch lost its passenger service on 31st December 1951 but the freight service lasted until 1st July 1963. Two small branch lines still in use for freight only are the Abingdon line, which closed to passengers on 9th September 1963, and Wallingford, closing to passengers on 15th June 1959. Both these branches used the traditional branch line train of the GWR with an auto trailer and 0-4-2T locomotive propelling and pulling. Near these two small lines, the one time Didcot, Newbury & Southampton Railway traversed the undulating Berkshire Hills southwards to Shawford Junction. Freight traffic was very heavy on this north to south line but was eventually diverted via Reading. The Didcot to Newbury & Southampton passenger service ceased on 10th September 1962 and freight terminated on 10th August 1964. Newbury was also the starting point for the Lambourn branch; a traditional GWR branch line which used GWR railcars and meandered through the Berkshire countryside passing 'pagoda' GWR halts en route. The line closed completely on 4th January 1960 to Welford Park from Lambourn. Welford Park to Newbury lasted until 5th November 1973 for freight traffic. Little visible evidence remains today of this once charming Great Western branch line. Station sites have been sold off, redeveloped, turned into industrial estates and the halts have been obliterated, making tracing the line today very difficult.

WILTSHIRE & BERKSHIRE

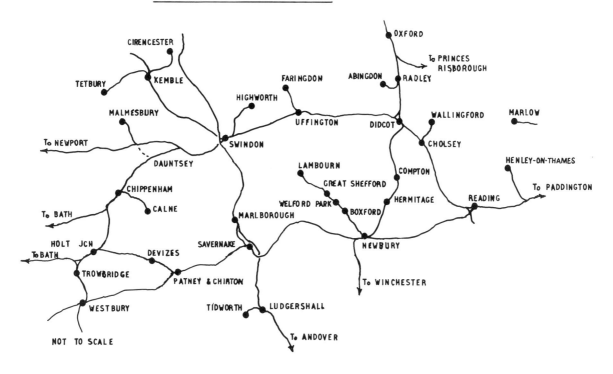

NOT TO SCALE

Plate 86: Malmesbury, on 3rd July 1960, showing the weeds slowly taking over the former passenger station which was closed on 10th September 1951. Freight lasted until 12th November 1962. In this picture, another feature, unique to the GWR can be seen: the rails on the loop are mounted on occasional cross ties with intermediate concrete blocks for the chairs. This was a wartime economy effected by the Permanent Way Engineer and carried out in sidings on the GWR, thereby saving valuable timber.

Plate 87: A platform scene at Lambourn, in December 1959, with GWR seats, platform trolleys and a handful of passengers. The site is now a housing estate, there being no trace of this station at all.

Plates 88 & 89: Lambourn, on 1st February 1958: a bleak midwinter scene with *(above)* an ex-GWR pannier tank and single coach. The line was usually worked by a GWR railcar. The station site has been sold and is now an industrial estate. *(Below)* The driver has been 'caught napping' reading the notice with his spectacles on. In fact, spectacles were issued to drivers by the Motive Power Department; a fact little known to the public! The station closed completely on 4th January 1960.

Plates 90 to 92: The Lambourn branch, on 12th December 195[...] just a few days before closure to passenger traffic. (Above) Gre[at] Shefford, with a Hawksworth bow-ended coach and an ex-GW[R] pannier tank. (Left) A close up of the nameboard and wooden fenci[ng] with its wire strands. (Below) Boxford, with the guard closing the doo[r] of the Hawksworth coach. The 'pagoda' corrugated iron hut is shown [in] detail as is the lamp hook and ratchet post for hoisting the oil lamps [at] night!

Plates 93 & 94: Hermitage *(above)* and Compton *(below)* on 23rd July 1962, with a single unit railcar working an afternoon Didcot to Newbury service. The crew wait patiently whilst the photographer finds the best position to photograph the station buildings and the train! The BR headcode is in use on the front of the vehicle. The station nameboards are of cast iron and both stations are oil-lit. The footbridge at Compton rather ruins the view. Hermitage, on the same line, is not considered worthy of a footbridge but both stations possess a commodious bicycle shed. Passenger services finished a few weeks later, on 10th September 1962 and freight ceased on 10th August 1964.

G. W. R.

Compton

Plate 95: Ex-GWR 14XX class, No. 1407 wheezes into Cholsey Station, on 21st February 1959, with the Wallingford train and a pre-war auto trailer. The GWR roundel has been cleaned on the otherwise dirty 14XX class tank photographed eleven years after nationalization! In this view, the steps to the auto coach can be clearly seen. These were lowered, by the guard, to enable passengers, at rail level halts, to board the train.

G.W.R.

Princes Risboro

TO

Abingdon

Plate 96: Wallingford, with ex-GWR 0-4-2T, No. 1407 at rest in the platform. The branch closed to passengers on 15th June 1959. Note the engine shed with lifted track and the GWR seats.

Midland and South Western Junction Railway.

(170)   [W. & S. Ltd.]

TIDWORTH

Plate 97: The Midland & South Western Junction Railway was a long cross-country line which rambled from Cheltenham to Andover and had its own station at Swindon. The GWR took over the line in 1923 but the SR had running powers. An ex-Southern Railway N class 2-6-0, No. 31816, can be seen with ex-works GWR stock. Behind the train are the old headquarters of the MSWJR.

Plate 98: Cirencester Watermoor sees an ex-Southern Railway U class 2-6-0, No. 31613, on a Cheltenham to Andover train in 1958. This station is now part of a town bypass road. *(Left)* An MSWJR label; the largest of any pre-group type, measuring 4¾in. x 2¼in., and printed by Waterlow & Sons.

Plate 99: Witham, in the summer of 1958, with an ex-works ex-GWR 'Hall' class locomotive arriving with a train for Paddington. Behind the footbridge the nameboard, informing the passenger to change for the Cheddar Valley line, a long meander across country to Yatton, on the Bristol line, can be seen. The line closed for passenger traffic on 9th September 1963. A GWR feature here is the lamp post for holding the oil lamp which would be wound up into place by the station staff before sunset, a ratchet being attached to the post for this purpose.

Plate 100: A glimpse, from the train window, of the signal box on the platform at Montacute. The guard is loading parcels from the brake van of the Hawksworth bow-ended stock, a feature of which was the non-slam locks which were peculiar to the GWR. The unwary passenger had to be careful when closing the door. The Taunton to Yeovil branch closed on 15th June 1964.

SOMERSET AND DORSET

The Great Western reached Bristol in 1840, connected with the Bristol & Exeter Railway, and was opened to Bridgwater in 1841. In 1847, the broad gauge branch was opened from Yatton to Clevedon, the first GWR branch, only 3¼ miles long. It still retained its broad gauge characteristics right up to closure to all traffic on 3rd October 1966. The station at Clevedon had an overall roof, a feature of Brunel's country stations in the West of England. The nearby Portishead branch closed to passenger traffic on 7th September 1964, the station having been completely rebuilt at Portishead in 1954. In North Somerset ran the Wrington Vale Light Railway which was Great Western-owned and which closed to passengers on 14th September 1931. The freight service was withdrawn on 1st November 1950 from Wrington, the section from Congresbury to Wrington closing on 10th June 1963. The Cheddar Valley branch from Yatton to Witham opened as the East Somerset Railway to Wells in 1862 and to Witham in 1874. The passenger service from Yatton to Witham ceased on 9th September 1963, freight services from Yatton to Cheddar ending on 1st October 1964 and from Cheddar to Cranmore on 1st April 1964. The section from Cranmore to Doulting, near Shepton Mallet, has been purchased by a preservation group called, appropriately enough, the East Somerset Railway.

The Bristol to Frome branch closed to passengers on 2nd November 1959, freight traffic over this line having ceased from Mells Road to Radstock on 25th April 1966, Radstock to Midsomer Norton on 1st June 1969, and Midsomer Norton to Bristol on 15th July 1968. The Bristol to Frome branch, known as the North Somerset line joined up at Hallatrow with a cross-country line to Limpley Stoke which closed as early as 21st September 1925. The Limpley Stoke to Camerton line remained open to freight until 15th February 1951 and was immortalized in the film 'The Titfield Thunderbolt' made on the branch in 1952.

In Dorset, the GWR had two traditional branch lines worked by auto trains. The Bridport branch traversed some very hilly countryside and closed completely on 5th May 1975, the freight to West Bay having ceased on 3rd December 1962. The passenger service to West Bay from Bridport finished on 22nd September 1930. The other Dorset branch, to Abbotsbury, closed to all traffic on 1st December 1952.

The broad gauge Bristol & Exeter Railway built a branch to Chard, a distance of 12½ miles, which opened in 1866, terminating at a station with an overall roof and shared with the standard gauge London & South Western branch. There was a cross platform interchange between the broad and standard gauge tracks. This platform was visible until the line was closed to passengers on 10th September 1962, freight ceasing on 6th July 1964. The nearby ex-broad gauge Taunton to Yeovil branch closed on the same day to all traffic.

The West Somerset Railway had a more happy ending than most lines as it has now re-opened as a tourist railway with steam trains running during the summer months for day trippers. The West Somerset line opened up for business from Taunton to Watchet on 31st March 1862, as a broad gauge line, the extension to Minehead following on 16th July 1874. The passenger service, operated by British Rail, terminated on 4th January 1971. Since then, the line has re-opened as a preserved line, using steam-hauled trains and was formally opened on 28th March 1976 from Minehead to Blue Anchor. The company hope, eventually, to run a regular passenger service from Taunton to Minehead.

The lengthy 43 mile cross-country branch from Taunton (Norton Fitzwarren) to Barnstaple Victoria Road was opened, as a broad gauge line, on 1st November 1873. The line ran in and out of Devon and dodged the Devon/Somerset borders en route. A connection was made with the Exe Valley branch at Dulverton. The GWR Barnstaple branch closed to all traffic on 3rd October 1966. Travelling over this line was a very pleasurable experience. Every station was built in the middle of nowhere at some distance from the nearest village. The 'gaffers' at stations seemed to be quite content with their lot and seemed to operate the signal box, booking office and goods depots all at the same time. The stations produced quite a few relics in tickets and other GWR memorabilia.

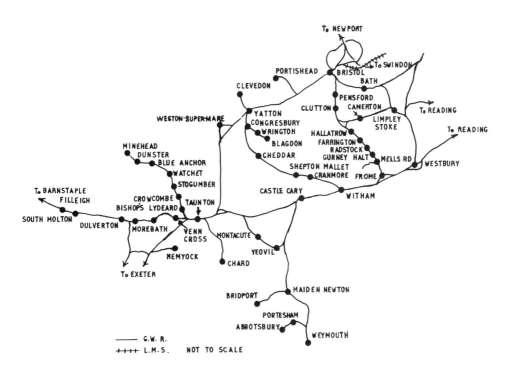

Plate 101: A driver's eye view of Martock which has been 'Southernized' with SR green paint and upper quadrant signals.

Plate 102: Clevedon, on 22nd June 1958: a branch line terminal of the former Bristol & Exeter Railway, opened in 1847 as a broad gauge branch from Yatton and closed on 3rd October 1966. The station buildings housed a small overall roof, but the platforms were lengthy to enable seaside excursion trains, from Bristol, to bring large crowds of day trippers to the town on summer Sundays. The space between the goods shed and the platform is more than adequate for the standard gauge tracks, but would suffice for a 7ft. 0¼in. platform line and run round loop.

ates 103 & 104: Scenes on the North Somerset branch, on 17th October 1959. *(Above)* Ex-GWR pannier tank, No. 3735 arrives at Pensford and the 'staff' is being ‸ought out for the locomotive crew whilst the guard hands a note over to the station ‸aster. The station seems to be bereft of passengers. *(Below)* Clutton sees a sprinkling of ‸ssengers. Note the spare headlamp on the side of the engine. This line closed to passen‸ ‸rs on 2nd November 1959.

G. W. R.

PENSFORD

G. W. R.

Midsomer Norton
AND WELTON

Plate 105: Farrington Gurney Halt, on the Bristol to Frome branch, was unique. The halt was unstaffed but tickets were obtainable from the 'Miner's Arms', seen behind the nameboard. Passengers wishing to obtain tickets for travel had to adjourn to the saloon bar and, during the process of consuming their pint, were able to select a ticket from behind the bar to their intended destination! Outside licencing hours passengers could purchase their tickets from a window in the side of the pub wall. There was a bell to arouse the landlord, or his staff, from afternoon slumber!

Plate 106: Chard Central, in the pouring rain, with ex-GWR pannier tank, No. 9671 about to take water. The line closed to passengers, from Taunton, on 10th September 1962. The freight traffic ceased on 6th July 1964.

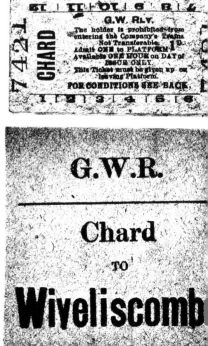

Plate 107: Weymouth Quay was another unusual branch line, as the trains ran through the streets, which was unusual in England. The trains were hauled by a special class of outside cylinder pannier tank; the 1366 class. Six of this class were built at Swindon in 1934. A member of the class, No. 1369, is preserved on the Dart Valley Railway.

Plate 108: The Bridport branch was worked by ex-GWR 14XX class 0-4-2 tanks. Here, No. 1403 is about to set out with a through train to Bridport from Weymouth. The auto train did not convey through passengers as it had to shunt, by gravity, at Maiden Newton to get on to the branch off the main line. The Bridport branch closed completely on 5th May 1975.

Plates 109 & 110: Milverton, with *(above)* ex-GWR Mogul, No. 6340 and *(below)* Mogul, No. 7337 arriving at Venn Cross on 9th July 1962. The Taunton to Barnstaple branch closed down to all traffic on 3rd October 1966. The line was opened on 1st November 1873 and was built to the broad gauge.

Plate 111: Morebath, on 9th July 1962, with ex-GWR Mogul, No. 7304 and GWR bow-ended Hawksworth coaches. The platform had been considerably extended to accommodate lengthy through trains which the Western Region ran on summer Saturdays.

Plate 112: Dulverton, on the Taunton to Barnstaple branch, which closed on 3rd October 1966. An Exe Valley branch train, headed by an ex-GWR pannier tank, waits in the bay on 14th June 1958. The coaches are red and cream early BR livery. The Exe Valley branch closed, from Thorverton to Morebath Junction, to both passengers and freight on 7th October 1963.

Plate 113: South Molton, with a Taunton to Barnstaple train, headed by ex-GWR 2-6-0, No. 6372. The branch, which was 43 miles long, closed completely on 7th October 1963.

Plate 114: Filleigh; with ex-GWR 2-6-0, No. 7304 making a brief stop at this remote GWR station on the former Taunton to Barnstaple line. This station still exists as a private house, owned by a Mr Joannes, an eccentric rustic, who practises self-sufficiency. The track has been lifted and filled in to form a lawn. Round the edge of the lawn are cages and pens where various animals and birds are kept to produce eggs and milk. Bed and breakfast is available, upon request, at a moderate fee and visitors can spend the night in the former booking office. The building is entirely gas-lit, there being no electricity supply. The owner also has a good selection of photographs of the branch to show to his visitors.

Plate 115: Dunster, with the short pick-up freight hauled by ex-GWR 0-6-0 pannier tank, No. 5798, about to do some leisurely shunting in the pouring rain, on 11th July 1962. This station is still in being as the line which closed, on 4th January 1971, has been re-opened by the West Somerset Railway.

Plate 116: Minehead, the terminus of the branch from Taunton, now known as the West Somerset Railway, with a B R Standard Class 3, 2-6-2 tank, No. 82044, on 11th July 1962. The station has changed very little and is still very similar today. Notice how the 'GWR' has been altered to 'WR' on the station seat!

Plates 117 & 118: Crowcombe, with before and after photographs of the summit station on the West Somerset Railway. *(Above)* The line as seen in the summer of 1962, with a B R Standard Class 3, 2-6-2 arriving from Minehead with GWR stock. *(Below)* In 1976, the line awaits restoration having been closed for five years and allowed to fall into disrepair.

Plates 119 & 120:   Stogumber, on the West Somerset branch, showing the contrasts between the line in its heyday and the scene of near dereliction after closure on 4th January 1971. *(Above)* In July 1962, ex-GWR 2-6-2T, No. 4143 arrives with a Taunton train. *(Below)* A view taken from the same spot fourteen years later; the ravages of time and Western Region rationalization have taken their toll. Gone are the camping coach in chocolate and cream, the water tank and stores van and even the signalling. The steps to the oil lamp holder still remain!

Plates 121 & 122: Another contrast between 'before' and 'after' showing *(above)* ex-GWR 2-6-2T, No. 4128 arriving, in July 1962, at Bishop's Lydeard, with a Taunton to Minehead train and *(below)* the scene after closure and before restoration, in 1976, showing the weedy track and some locomotives purchased by the West Somerset Railway. The broad gauge goods shed remains virtually unaltered in this 1976 picture.

DEVON & CORNWALL

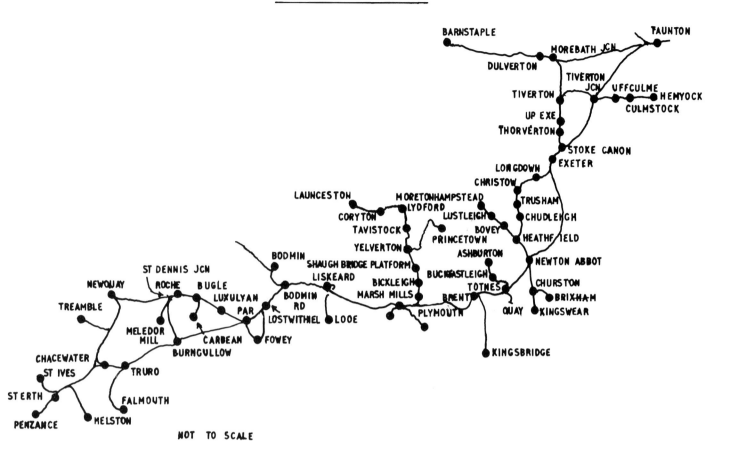

NOT TO SCALE

DEVON AND CORNWALL

The broad gauge main line reached Penzance in 1867. The West Cornwall Railway was, however, opened as a standard gauge concern to Penzance in 1852 and converted to mixed gauge by 1st March 1867. Broad gauge lines were constructed until 1877, the last branch to be built on the GWR to have broad gauge being the St. Ives branch, on 1st June 1877. The St. Ives branch was converted to standard gauge in May 1892. After having established a main line route over the Bristol & Exeter, South Devon, Cornwall and West Cornwall Railways to Penzance, branch lines soon followed.

The Taunton to Barnstaple branch was opened on 1st November 1873 and was broad gauge. The line closed to all traffic on 30th October 1966. The picturesque Exe Valley line, worked by auto trains and 14XX class 0-4-2 tanks until its closure, closed completely on 7th October 1963 from Thorverton to Morebath Junction, and for passengers between Dulverton and Exeter. Thorverton to Stoke Canon, on the main line, closed to freight on 30th November 1966. The cross-country Tiverton to Tiverton Junction line, also worked by push-pull trains, closed to all traffic on 5th June 1967, passenger trains having ceased on 5th October 1964. The tortuous Hemyock branch closed to freight traffic on 3rd November 1976. The passenger service over the Hemyock

branch ceased on 9th September 1963. The line was opened on 29th May 1876 as the Culm Valley Light Railway and the trains were so slow that British Railways had to use gas-lit vehicles to light the trains as the electric lighting could not be generated by conventional means. The gas-lit coaches of former Barry Railway origin finished work on 9th September 1963 at the closure of the line. They were the last gas-lit vehicles in use on the Western Region and possibly on British Railways as a whole.

South of Exeter, the Teign Valley branch wove an inland course, via Heathfield, to Newton Abbot, the main line taking the sea route via Dawlish. The Teign Valley was a line that passed through very picturesque countryside and possessed some unspoilt stations. One station was not even served by a public road, the only access being by public footpath through woodland. The entire stock of tickets at Longdown in the summer of 1957, was Great Western; not one single ticket was post-nationalization. The line was closed to passengers on 9th June 1958 and freight was withdrawn from Exeter to Christow on the same day, from Christow to Trusham on 1st May 1961 and from Trusham to Heathfield on 4th December 1967.

Passengers for Ashburton boarded their trains at Totnes and trundled along the Dart Valley line, where passenger services

Plate 123: Moorswater, in June 1958, shows the contrast between the Looe branch and the main line. An ex-GWR 'Castle' class locomotive crosses the viaduct with the 'up' 'Cornish Riviera'. Note the old piers from the Brunel structure which was wooden-tiered and replaced in the 1930s. In the foreground, an ex-GWR 55XX class 2-6-2T sits outside the old Liskeard & Looe shed which, at the time of this photograph, had an engine road compiled of old bridgerail dating from the broad gauge era.

C.R.

Passenger Luggage.

Bodmin Road tc

Launcestn

were withdrawn on 3rd November 1958, freight being disco tinued on 10th September 1962. The line partly re-opened the Dart Valley Railway, using steam power, on 5th Ap 1969. The section from Buckfastleigh to Ashburton w obliterated by a new road but this was a blessing in disgui as the new road now brings tourists to visit the railway.

Another South Devon branch line that was not so lucky w the Moretonhampstead branch. The GWR kept a large hot at Moretonhampstead which was always shown on the GW carriage maps. The branch opened as a South Devon broa gauge concern in 1866 and closed to passengers on 2nd Marc 1959. The freight service from Mortonhampstead to Bove ceased on 6th April 1964 and from Bovey to Heathfield 4th May 1970. Heathfield to Newton Abbot is still in u today for oil traffic.

The Torbay & Dartmouth Railway steams away eve summer between Paignton and Kingswear and uses ex-GW engines painted in their Brunswick Green livery and has rolli stock painted in the chocolate and cream livery. From th main line once ran the short Churston to Brixham branc worked by auto trains from a special bay at Churston. Th short branch closed to all traffic on 13th May 1963. T Kingsbridge branch closed to all traffic on 16th Septemb 1963, a sad loss to railway enthusiasts as with all Dev branch lines, it was so picturesque. Another rare line in Dev was the Princetown branch which closed to all traffic on 5 March 1956. This line had the distinction of being the highe above sea level on the former GWR system, and ran acro open moorland through some very bleak countryside.

The Launceston to Plymouth branch, which connecte with the Princetown branch at Yelverton, closed to passenge on 31st December 1962. The freight traffic over this li finally ceased between Launceston and Lydford on 28 February 1966. Lydford to Tavistock South closed to freig on 7th September 1964, Tavistock South to Marsh Mi having closed on 31st December 1962 to all traffic. T Plymouth to Yealmpton line closed completely on 29 February 1960, the passenger service having been withdraw by the GWR on 6th October 1947.

In Cornwall, the china clay traffic is flourishing and so a the branch lines although it is not now possible to trav through from St. Dennis Junction to Burngullow. The line Gunheath and Carbean closed, on 29th April 1965, to freig traffic. The Looe branch still exists although greatly ration ized, but the Fowey branch was closed to passengers on 4 January 1965. The passenger service from Fowey to S Blazey ceased on 8th July 1929 and the branch closed freight on 1st July 1968.

Nearer to Penzance, the Helston branch closed on 5 November 1962, to passengers, and on 5th October 1964 freight. The Newquay to Chacewater branch closed on 4 February 1963 to passengers and to freight on 28th Octob 1963. Bodmin still sees a little freight: this being china clay Wenford which runs over the former Southern route v Boscarne Junction. The GWR line from Bodmin Road Nanstallon, ceased to operate for passengers on 30th Janua 1967. The GWR mineral branch from Shepherds to Treamb closed on 1st January 1952. On the whole, Cornwall suffer less regarding closures compared with other parts of t country.

Plates 124 to 126: Scenes on the Exe Valley Railway on 10th July 1962. *(Above)* GWR 0-4-2T, No. 1462 whisks away from Up Exe Halt en route to Exeter with a double coach auto train. *(Below)* The same locomotive is seen arriving at Tiverton from Exeter. The line closed to passengers on 7th October 1963. *(Right)* Two relics are shown: a GWR luggage label to the Highland Railway, with the route shown in great detail, and a GWR season ticket, used until 14th June 1958.

(135a)

GREAT WESTERN RAILWAY.

TIVERTON JUNCTION

TO

(HIGH. RLY.)

CARRIAGE, PAID.

Route via CREWE, L. & N.W.R., LANC., CARLISLE, PERTH, and DUNKELD.

G.W.R.   G.W.R.
WEEKLY   **19**   THIRD
SEASON   CLASS

No. 1563   EXPIRES   Rate 7/7

14 JUN 1958

BETWEEN

TIVERTON (DEVON) &

TIVERTON JUNCTION

G.W.R.

Brixham

G.W.R.

IDE

Plate 127: Brixham, with ex-GWR 0-4-2T, No. 1452 and single coach auto trailer bound for Churston on 1st November 1958. The Western Region auto trailers were built until 1954 and were the last non-standard coaches built for British Railways. The branch closed to all traffic on 13th May 1963.

Plate 128: Chudleigh, on the Teign Valley Railway, was a rural backwater of the Western Region and is seen here, on 24th August 1957, with ex-GWR 0-4-2T, No. 1438 approaching. The line closed to passengers on 9th June 1958. Notice the hanging baskets of flowers at the station; a regular GWR feature.

G.W.R.

Trusham

G.W.R.

Heathfield

Plates 129 & 130: Scenes on the Culm Valley Light Railway or Hemyock branch with ex-GWR 0-4-2T, No. 1450 and milk tanks at *(above)* Hemyock and *(below)* Culmstock. The locomotive displays the appropriate headcode for the train on the front buffer beam. This particular locomotive can still be seen at work on the nearby Dart Valley Railway, and it is now named *Ashburton*.

Plates 131 & 132: Ex-GWR 0-4-2T, No. 1450, is seen working the milk empties at Uffculme on 23rd August 1964. The passenger service over the branch finished on 9th September 1963 and the freight ceased on 3rd November 1975. *(Below right)* A label from Hemyock to Mitre Bridge, near Willesden; the destination for the milk tanks which came off the branch.

(18
BRITISH RLYS. (WESTERN REG

HEMYOCK
TO
MITRE BRIDGE, L.M

No. of Packages		CARRIAGE PAID

Route via KENSINGTON

Plates 133 & 134: The Ashburton branch was worked by ex-GWR 14XX class 0-4-2Ts from Totnes and was opened as a broad gauge branch of the South Devon Railway on 1st May 1872. No. 1470 is seen *(above)* on 20th April 1957 sitting beneath the overall roof at Ashburton. *(Below)* The last day on the branch, 1st November 1958, with 14XX class locomotives Nos. 1466 and 1470 leaving Buckfastleigh: a scene now considerably changed.

Plates 135 & 136:   Ashburton branch scenes, on 1st November 1958. *(Above)* The 5-coach branch train is seen approaching Totnes double-headed by ex-GWR 0-4-2Ts Nos. 1466 and 1470; a very rare sight. *(Below)* The train is seen arriving at Staverton, now called Staverton Bridge. Freight on the line ceased on 10th September 1962, but the line re-opened as the Dart Valley Railway on 5th April 1969, but only from Buckfastleigh to Totnes. *(Right)* A South Devon Railway label obtainable at the time of closure.

(96)

S. D. R.

Passenger's Luggage.

Staverton to

Lidford

ate 137: A view of Staverton Station showing the layout and crossing, on 1st
*ovember 1958.

ate 138: Kingsbridge sees an ex-GWR 45XX class 2-6-2 tank, No. 4568, on 20th April
*57. The line closed to all traffic on 16th September 1963. Note the broad gauge
*rriage shed still in use on the left. *(Right)* A South Devon Railway label from Staverton.

Plates 139 to 141: Moretonhampstead, on 20th April 1957. *(Above)* Ex-GWR 2-6-2T, No. 5138 runs round the train under the overall roof in this view taken from the cattle dock. *(Below)* No. 5183 is ready to depart and passengers start to appear, including a youthful John Phillips. *(Right)* The commemoration stone of the opening of the broad gauge branch in 1866. This stone is now in the National Collection. The line closed to passengers on 2nd March 1959 and to freight on 6th April 1964. *(Below and bottom right)* Luggage labels from the South Devon and Cornwall railways.

844

C.R.

Bodmin Road to

MORETONHAMPSTEAD

96   **S.D.R.**

Passenger Luggage.

Lustleigh to

KINGSWEAR

Plates 142 & 143: Lustleigh, on the Moretonhampstead branch, on 20th April 1957, with *(above)* ex-GWR 2-6-2T No. 5183 bound for Newton Abbot and *(below)* a general view of the station buildings from the road bridge. The station still had S D R luggage labels in the rack at the time. In fact, the South Devon Railway was taken over by the Great Western in 1878. Passenger services ceased on 2nd March 1959.

96   **S.D.R.**

Passenger Luggage.

Lustleigh to

BRENT

S.D.R.

Passenger Luggage.

Lustleigh to

BRIDGEWATER

Plate 144: Bickleigh, with ex-GWR 2-6-2T, No. 5568 on a Launceston to Plymouth train, on 3rd April 1962. The two coaches are auto train trailers with drop down steps for rail level halts.

Plate 145: Yelverton, the junction for the Princetown branch, on 3rd April 1962. In this view, it is reduced in status to an unstaffed halt. Passengers for the Princetown branch commenced their journey from a separate bay platform through the entrance on the right. The Princetown branch closed to all traffic on 5th March 1956. Passenger services on the Launceston to Plymouth GWR line ceased on 31st December 1962.

Plate 146: Coryton Halt with an ex-GWR 2-6-2T, No. 5569, the standard type of GWR passenger locomotive for cross-country and branch lines. A total of 175 of this class was built, to a Churchward design, between 1906 and 1929, some of the class having square side tanks. This view was photographed on 3rd April 1962.

Plates 147 & 148: A view of a small country halt, Shaugh Bridge Platform, with 'pagoda' waiting hut, so beloved of the GWR. *(Below right)* Some interesting tickets were available in the late 1950s. The first shows the stage from London to Exeter with a free pass to the Southern Region 'frontier' at Exeter. Then an 'extension' ticket to Launceston is shown. An extension ticket was a ticket used to extend a journey, usually at night, when the booking office was closed. Next, a GWR-style Western Region single to Plymouth, routed via Marsh Mills, a BR blank card, and a GWR single to Exeter. A short trip up the Ashburton branch also produced a GWR return.

Plate 149: Churchward introduced the 2-6-0 Moguls to the GWR in 1911 and they were built until 1932. This clean and polished example is seen, in June 1958, on a Newquay portion of one of the through trains from Paddington. No. 6397 is seen hauling chocolate and cream Mk I stock near St. Dennis Junction.

Plate 150: St. Dennis Junction sees ex-GWR 57XX class 0-6-0 pannier tank, No. 9755 on a trip from the Meledor Mill branch, on 16th June 1958. There was more of this class of locomotive built by the GWR than any other and, in fact, some were built after nationalization up until 1955.

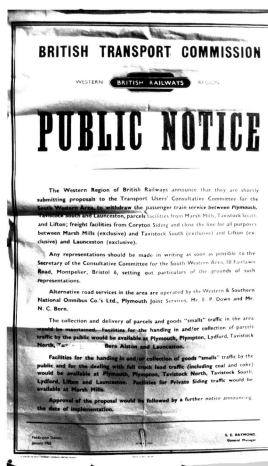

BRITISH TRANSPORT COMMISSION

WESTERN BRITISH RAILWAYS REGION

PUBLIC NOTICE

The Western Region of British Railways announce that they are shortly submitting proposals to the Transport Users' Consultative Committee for the South Western Area, to withdraw the passenger train service between Plymouth, Tavistock South and Launceston, parcels facilities from Marsh Mills, Tavistock South and Lifton; freight facilities from Coryton Siding and close the line for all purposes between Marsh Mills (exclusive) and Tavistock South (exclusive) and Lifton (exclusive) and Launceston (exclusive).

Any representations should be made in writing as soon as possible to the Secretary of the Consultative Committee for the South Western Area, 10 Fairlawn Road, Montpelier, Bristol 6, setting out particulars of the grounds of such representations.

Alternative road services in the area are operated by the Western & Southern National Omnibus Co.'s Ltd., Plymouth Joint Services, Mr. E. P. Down and Mr. N. C. Born.

The collection and delivery of parcels and goods "smalls" traffic in the area would be maintained. Facilities for the handing in and/or collection of parcels traffic by the public would be available at Plymouth, Plympton, Lydford, Tavistock North, Tavistock South, Bere Alston and Launceston.

Facilities for the handing in and/or collection of goods "smalls" traffic by the public and for the dealing with full truck load traffic (including coal and coke) would be available at Plymouth, Plympton, Tavistock North, Tavistock South, Lydford, Lifton and Launceston. Facilities for Private Siding traffic would be available at Marsh Mills.

Approval of the proposal would be followed by a further notice announcing the date of implementation.

Paddington Station,
January 1962

S. E. RAYMOND,
General Manager

Plate 151: At Luxulyan, on 20th June 1958, an ex-GWR 51XX class 2-6-2T, No. 5193 eases out of the station with an evening train to Newquay. The train comprises GWR compartment stock in BR maroon livery.

Plate 152: On 28th June 1958 at St. Dennis Junction, on the Par to Newquay line, stands ex-GWR 4200 class 2-8-0 mineral tank, No. 4294. Designed by Churchward, and built from 1910, the 42XX class of which this is one, consisted of 205 locomotives. They were used mainly in South Wales. Alongside No. 4294 is No. 5519, a 2-6-2T with gleaming brass safety valve. In the background can be seen the china clay spoil heaps so common to this part of Cornwall.

Plates 153 & 154: Another famous GWR class of locomotive was the small 2-6-2 tank, used for branch line work, of which No. 4552 is an example. *(Above)* This locomotive is seen skidding to a halt on the Nanstallon branch with china clay wagons. *(Below)* No. 5557, of the same class, but with tapered side tanks, rushes along near St. Dennis Junction on the Par to Newquay branch. Note the wooden 'staff' halt and the fireman with his hand out to pick up the 'staff'.

844a   **W.C.R.**

Passenger Luggage.

Scorrier to

Perranwel

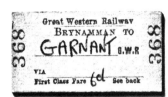

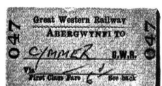
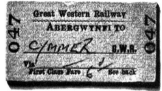

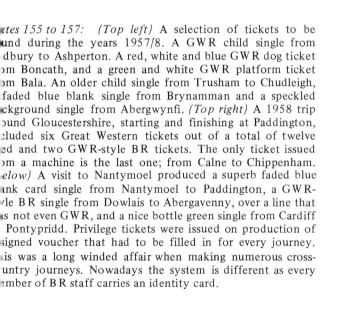

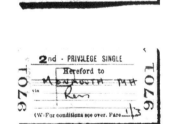

Plates 155 to 157: (Top left) A selection of tickets to be found during the years 1957/8. A GWR child single from Ledbury to Ashperton. A red, white and blue GWR dog ticket from Boncath, and a green and white GWR platform ticket from Bala. An older child single from Trusham to Chudleigh, a faded blue blank single from Brynamman and a speckled background single from Abergwynfi. *(Top right)* A 1958 trip round Gloucestershire, starting and finishing at Paddington, included six Great Western tickets out of a total of twelve used and two GWR-style BR tickets. The only ticket issued from a machine is the last one; from Calne to Chippenham. *(Below)* A visit to Nantymoel produced a superb faded blue blank card single from Nantymoel to Paddington, a GWR-style BR single from Dowlais to Abergavenny, over a line that was not even GWR, and a nice bottle green single from Cardiff to Pontypridd. Privilege tickets were issued on production of a signed voucher that had to be filled in for every journey. This was a long winded affair when making numerous cross-country journeys. Nowadays the system is different as every member of BR staff carries an identity card.

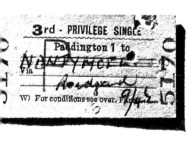

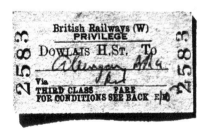

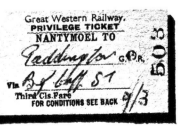

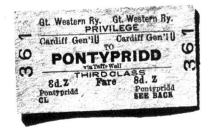

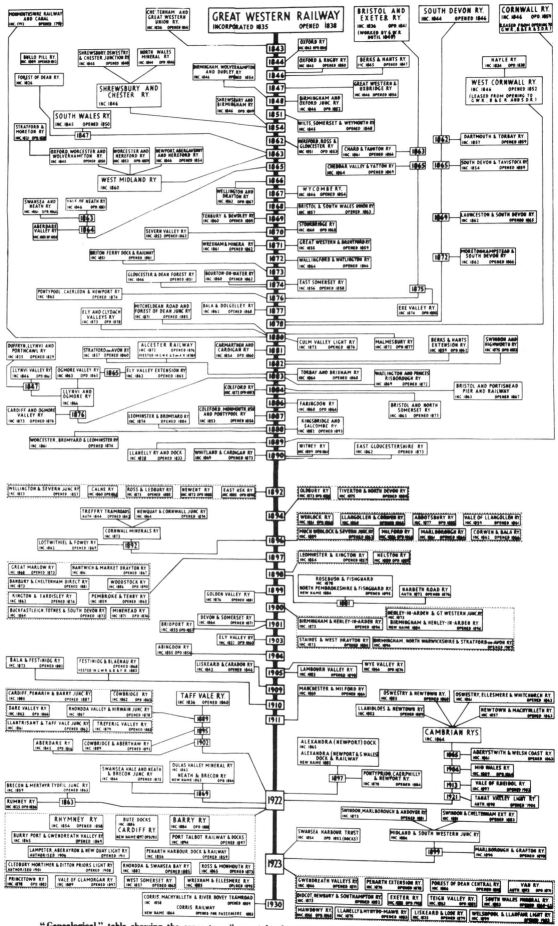

"Genealogical" table showing the separate railway and other companies absorbed by the Great Western Railway

INDEX TO LOCATIONS FEATURED IN THIS ALBUM

NOTE: Although certain locations listed in this index are not geographically situated in the counties under which they fall, they have been included therein as the pictures fall in sections which cross county borders.